DO
THE NEW
YOU

DO
THE NEW
YOU

6 MINDSETS
TO BECOME WHO YOU
WERE CREATED TO BE

STEVEN FURTICK

Faith
Words

NEW YORK   NASHVILLE

FaithWords
Hachette Book Group
1290 Avenue of the Americas, New York, NY 10104
faithwords.com
twitter.com/faithwords

First edition: February 2024

FaithWords is a division of Hachette Book Group, Inc. The FaithWords name and logo are trademarks of Hachette Book Group, Inc.

The publisher is not responsible for websites (or their content) that are not owned by the publisher.

FaithWords books may be purchased in bulk for business, educational, or promotional use. For information, please contact your local bookseller or the Hachette Book Group Special Markets Department at special.markets@hbgusa.com.

Library of Congress Cataloging-in-Publication Data has been applied for.

ISBNs: 9781546006824 (hardcover), 9781546007777 (trade pbk. intl.), 9781546007081 (ebook)

Printed in the United States of America

LSC-H

Printing 1, 2023

For Mom, you turned pinecones to platinum.

CONTENTS

MINDSET (01)

I'M NOT STUCK UNLESS I STOP.
ACTION STEP: COMMIT TO PROGRESS.

MINDSET (02)

CHRIST IS IN ME. I AM ENOUGH.
ACTION STEP: ACCEPT YOUR SELF.

MINDSET (06)

GOD HAS GIVEN ME EVERYTHING I NEED FOR THE SEASON I'M IN.

ACTION STEP: EMBRACE YOUR NOW.

THE TRAP, THE TREADMILL, AND THE TRUE YOU

A week before he left for college, my oldest son asked me a question. "Out of everything you've taught me, what's the best advice you can give me right now?"

In that moment, no profound answer came to my mind. The very idea of "the best" advice freaks me out a little, like I'm expected to condense the world's wisdom into a sentence and chisel it onto a stone tablet. I'm not Moses.

I don't know the best advice, but I do know what the worst advice would have been.

"Just do you."

Okay, maybe it's not the absolute worst advice in the world, but it's up there. Why? Because "you" is someone you haven't fully met yet. Certainly not by the time you graduate high school. And, if we're honest, probably not any time soon after that.

"Doing you" is about being yourself, but do you really know yourself when you're eighteen? Or twenty-eight? Or eighty, for that matter? Often, your self-perception is mostly made up of your life experience so far, which leads you to a belief about the way things are and always will be.

Don't get me wrong: I'm not saying *don't* do you. I'm not saying to be somebody else. Being your full, authentic, unique self is a solid goal to strive for and a healthy place to be. And letting go of the pressure of constantly comparing yourself to others is liberating. So I'm all in favor of self-acceptance. Who else would you be, after all?

> If you overcommit to your concept of who you are today, it closes you off to what you could become tomorrow.

And yet, if you overcommit to your concept of who you are today, it closes you off to what you could become tomorrow. That's the problem with just "doing you."

It doesn't set you free. It keeps you frozen.

It's not self-awareness. It's self-sabotage.

It's not the truth. It's a trap.

THE TREADMILL

I think most of us instinctively realize, sooner or later, that "just doing you" isn't enough. Who we've been up until this point can only get us so far. I'm sure that there are some things about yourself you want to tweak, and a few others you want to completely transform. I know there are for me.

So here's what we usually do. We escape the "do you" trap, only to climb onto the "future you" treadmill—which turns out to be almost as limiting and even more exhausting.

What is future you? It's you, but with greater faith, better friends, a flatter stomach, total financial freedom, and near-absolute perfection in every moment, forever and ever, amen. Future you is the shiny, perfect version of you. It's who you wish you could be. Who you think you should be. Who you would be if you just tried a little harder.

After chasing future you for a while and never quite catching it, you're left exhausted, and often a little embarrassed. But don't worry—there's always another course, product, diet, plan, church service, or New Year's resolution promising that *this time*, you'll really become future you. So you stay on the treadmill, running in place, pursuing a goal that's just out of reach.

Meanwhile, days, weeks, months, and years are slipping by, but you can't fully enjoy them because you're out of breath, chasing the person you think you could be. The person you would be proud of. The person who will finally be worthy of acceptance, success, love, fulfillment.

The problem, of course, is that future you is largely an illusion. It's a mirage that stays just out of reach. And often, that vision doesn't even come from inside of you. It's more like a highlight reel of everyone else's supposed strengths and successes. You only see their highlights, though. You don't know what's hidden inside them—or hidden inside you.

If *doing you* is a trap that keeps you from growth, *future you* is a treadmill that kills contentment. If you are constantly working from the assumption that you need to become something you're not, you'll never be happy with who you are today, and you might die trying to produce something that was never put in you to begin with.

THE TRUE YOU

So, if *doing you* has left you stuck, and *future you* has left you discouraged, where should you turn? Where should the pursuit of self-identity and self-acceptance lead you?

To the *true you.*

The you God created you to be. The person he knows, sees, and believes in. That person includes who you are today, but it isn't stuck there. It probably encompasses many of the yearnings and dreams you have for the future, but it isn't frustrated by the fact that you're not there yet.

I believe with all my heart that God wants you to see yourself as he sees you, which is a lot more fully than you see yourself. Then, he wants to help you live out that God-given identity. That is the heart of this book: to help you align your mindsets with God's vision for you so you can live the most authentic version of yourself.

> Align your mindsets with God's vision for you so you can live the most authentic version of yourself.

After all, you haven't fully met you yet. But God has. He met that version of you because he made that version of you. The truth of you is still unfolding to you, but it is fully known by God.

Only God sees past the personality you've displayed so far, past the circumstances you've experienced that helped shape today's edition of you, all the way back to the person he created you to be. God has known you since before you were born. He knows what he put in you and what he's calling out of you.

When God called Jeremiah to be a prophet, he first had to convince Jeremiah that he was enough for his prophetic ministry. Jeremiah was having a tough time seeing beyond the person he had been up to that point. God said, "Before I formed you in the womb I knew you, before you were born I set you apart; I appointed you as a prophet to the nations" (Jeremiah 1:5).

Jeremiah didn't see himself as a prophet: he thought he was too young, too weak, too scared. But God told him, "I knew you before."

Think about that.

Before.

He knew Jeremiah before he was born, before the world had hurt him, before people had mocked him or fear had silenced him.

God knew the real Jeremiah because he created him. So he said, "Jeremiah, listen to me. I imagined you. I formed you. I set you apart. I appointed you, and I'm going to be with you. What more do you need?" When Jeremiah believed that, it changed everything.

It will do the same for you.

God knew you before. He knew you before you were born. He knew you before this world got ahold of you. He knew you before depression set in. He knew you before false accusations threatened you. He knew you before you were abused and abandoned. Long before the mistake, before the failure, before the addiction, God said, "I knew you."

He. Knew. You.

He knew you'd be in financial difficulty. He knew you'd have trouble getting pregnant. He knew you'd be struggling with your health. He knew you'd be dealing with depression. He knew you'd need a job. He knew the challenges your marriage would go through and the needs your kids would face.

He knew it all and he saw it all. And he declared, "I have plans for you. I have a place for you. I have a purpose for you."

The you he sees is the one who is still kicking, still going, still holding on. It's the you just waiting to break forth. It's the you who is coming up alive. It's the you this world won't corrupt. It's the you drama didn't distract and trauma couldn't kill.

You were fashioned and formed by a God whose creativity knows no end. He says that you were fearfully and wonderfully made, that he knit you together in the womb, that your days are written in his book. He is a God who counts the stars and calls them all by name. He numbers the hairs on your head and sees the life span of every sparrow. His knowledge of you is as specific as it is infinite. It encompasses everything from hairs to sparrows to stars, so it definitely includes you—every part of you, including the parts that you don't know yet and the parts you called a mistake.

God knew you before he created you, like he knew Jeremiah, and the you he knew is the you he is calling to the surface. You're the same person, but it's a new version, a fresh iteration, a greater understanding, a fuller experience, and an expanded definition of you.

The *new* you is the you God *knew*.

> His knowledge of you is as specific as it is infinite. It encompasses everything from hairs to sparrows to stars, so it definitely includes you—every part of you, including the parts that you don't know yet and the parts you called a mistake.

And that's the real you.

It might be unknown to you, at least in part and at least so far, but it's been known to God since before he created you.

Learning to "do the new you" gets you out of the trap of doing you and off the treadmill of future you. You don't have to settle for less than you are, and you don't have to strive to be what you're not. You just have to see yourself as God sees you and then walk in that "new you."

Are you ready to get out of the trap? Out of the thought patterns and default settings of your past? Out of the present-day story where you see yourself as a slave to your personality and programming?

Are you ready to get off the treadmill? No more wasted days making yourself miserable by measuring yourself against an ideal, an unrealistic version of a person God didn't create you to be to begin with? No more waiting to feel worthy or killing yourself to live up to something that's beyond you?

It's possible. But it's not always simple. I wish I could tell you there was a one-time decision you could make to accept yourself as you are right now, weaknesses and all, while simultaneously growing into the next level of strength God has for you. But it doesn't work that way. The true you is always trying to break through, but it's a breakthrough that isn't without tension. It's a tension I'm all too familiar with.

I know the tension of living with who I am now and wishing and wanting to become what I know I was meant to be all along. I know the embarrassment of not living up to my expectations for my own maturity when I've gotten stressed or angry. Times when I know I'm capable of doing more, of getting it right, and yet once again I've fallen short. It can feel so confusing, so contradictory.

I've had moments when I shared wisdom with my oldest son while we were lifting weights together, and I felt like Yoda, Warren Buffett, and Billy Graham all rolled into one. But then I've had other moments where I felt more like Homer Simpson.

I've had moments like the one where I took my daughter to see *Hamilton* in New York, and we created a tournament bracket of the best *Hamilton* songs, and I told myself she'd probably never find a man as good as me. But I've also had moments where I hoped to God she would never marry someone as impatient and irritable as I can be.

I've had both.

We've all had both.

We're all familiar with the trap of doing you and the treadmill of future you. I'm sure you've had moments of breakthrough followed by moments of breakdown, but the breakthroughs serve a purpose. They let you know it's possible to become that person you glimpsed ahead. Not just occasionally either. Not just once in a while.

That person you see is the *real you* breaking through.

Think about that. Let yourself believe that.

The moments when you act on an instinct to be generous. The moments where you choose freedom over addiction. The moments where you choose compassion over judgment. The moments where instead of sliding into self-destructive behavior, you actually do the thing that you know is going to make you feel better at the end of the day.

Have you had those moments? Do you feel a tugging toward something that God is doing within you? Do you sense that there is more inside you than you have seen up until now? That's what we are talking about in this book— that tension. That space. That gap between who you are today and where God is taking you.

Those breakthrough moments are reminders that you were created in the image of God to do good works, and the true you, the new you, is letting you know, "I'm here. I'm ready. I'm waiting. This is your invitation. Let's go!"

In this book, I'm going to share six mindsets, six affirmations, to put deep into your spirit. I want you to have a voice in your head that sounds more like the Holy Spirit and less like your old habits. Think of them as six downloads from heaven to update your mind and refresh your life. Some of it might feel unfamiliar to you, but it's been in you all along. It just hasn't taken root yet. Some of it you're already doing, but God wants you to experience more of it.

The advice I would give my son is the message I'm excited to share with you.

Don't settle for just "doing you." And don't waste another day chasing "future you."

The new you is not waiting in the future.

You can walk into it right now.

ONE

THE (K)NEW YOU

WHICH ME WILL I BE?

Every day around 6:00 a.m. when my alarm summons, the decisions begin.

Scroll mindlessly for fifteen minutes or open my Bible app and read the next chapter? One cup of coffee or two? (Because zero cups is not an option.) Black T-shirt or . . . black T-shirt? (Because most days, I'm pretty boring when it comes to my wardrobe.) Brush my teeth and then make the bed, or the other way around? Gratitude journal first, or prayer? Cold shower like that guy on YouTube suggested, or hot shower, like a normal human?

Options fly a mile a minute through my mind. I really should get this morning routine nailed down. The decisions are overwhelming and I'm barely out of bed.

I walk into the kitchen. Should I ignore the dishes in the sink or do them? Mutter about my kids being helpless and lazy or approach this simple act of responsible fatherhood as a quiet martyr? I hear them arguing upstairs, pushing each other's buttons with professional precision, inventing issues to fight about that would impress a politician. How will I respond? By yelling at them to stop yelling, or by staying in grown-up mode, knowing that no problem can be solved by matching the level of teenage hormonal energy that created it?

I have a to-do list I wrote out on a legal pad, I have kids with schedules they never write out, and I have a wife who deserves all of me. I have a staff to lead, a sermon to write, a songwriting session I'm low-key dreading and simultaneously anticipating because I don't know if we'll get anything good . . . but what if we do? I'm seeing the day through a thin residue of regret from things I didn't mean to say yesterday or kindness I meant to extend but couldn't quite get to come out of my mouth.

Sometimes my mind feels like one of the anthills we used to kick over in my grandmother's yard when we went to visit in the fall. Back then, we'd run away from the ants, but there's nowhere to run from the constant movement in my mind. I guess that's why psychologists call it ANTS syndrome: Automatic Negative Thinking. All I did was wake up and start thinking about my day, and the tunnels started collapsing, and now the ANTS are after me.

Permeating the decisions and doubts, the regrets and res-olutions, the plans and preoccupations, there is a decision I must make. It's the bigger decision, the one that shapes all the others.

Which me will I be?

Life shifts and slides, sometimes subtly, sometimes sud-denly. Which version of me will I bring to the next stage of my development? Will it be the me who is wiser from the wounds of yesterday, or the me who is trapped in the bit-terness of resentment and the guilt of regret?

Who will answer the door when temptations knock and a voice in my head whispers, *No one will know, you deserve it, it's not that bad*? The me who is focused on what I truly want, which is to be close to God and honor him in all my ways, or the me who is fixated on what I crave now: pleasure, escape, relief?

Which me will I bring to this struggle?

Which me will I bring to this moment?

Which me will I bring to this season?

It's the choice you face too. Which *you* will you do? Whether by default or design, you make this decision every moment, in every situation, in every relationship, at the open door of every opportunity and the closed door of every disappointment. You choose who to be and how to show up.

The other day I was on my way to the recording studio for a songwriting session. I had a lyric in my head that I didn't want to forget, so I recorded a voice memo while I drove. It went like this: "Jesus, please be patient with me. I'm so far from the person I want to be."

Which you will you do?

The exact moment I finished singing that line into my phone, somebody cut me off in traffic. Without thinking, I yelled, "Idiot!"

Of course the guy didn't hear me, but my phone was still recording. So now I had a voice memo that went, "Jesus, please be patient with me. I'm so far from the person I want to be. IDIOT!"

The irony was obvious. I couldn't even write a song about being a work in progress without interrupting my song to prove how much progress I still needed to make.

I often feel so far from the person I want to be. From the person I know God sees in me. From the person I'm capable of being, but must choose to be, over and over again.

That's why it is imperative that you see who you are *capable* of being, not just who you've always been. That you catch a glimpse of the you God sees, not just the you that you've always known.

> Catch a glimpse of the you God sees, not just the you that you've always known.

GOD KNOWS THAT YOU ... DO YOU?

In this book, I'm using the term "new you" to describe the concept of the truest, most authentic version of you. The one God sees in you. The phrase is inspired by a passage in Ephesians that talks about seeing this God-created version of you and then making it a reality. Paul wrote to the church in Ephesus:

> You were taught, with regard to your former way of life, to put off your old self, which is being corrupted by its deceitful desires; to be made new in the attitude of your minds; and to put on the new self, created to be like God in true righteousness and holiness. (4:22–24)

In other words, there is an old self and a new self. There is an old way of doing you, and there is a new way of doing you.

Now, I'm not saying the "old you" is a horrible, awful worm of a person. This isn't a book about hating yourself. But the old you isn't you at your *best*. It was you surviving. It was you reacting. It was you living according to your view of who you were and what you could do, but that view was based on your perspective.

There's so much more to you than that.

There is a God-empowered way of doing you, and that is you at your best. That's the you he created and the you he sees. That person might feel new to you, but it's not new at all.

Remember what God told Jeremiah? "Before I formed you in the womb *I knew you* . . ." God was asking Jeremiah to put off the old way of seeing himself and put on a new one. The old Jeremiah was small, scared, and quiet. The new Jeremiah was called to preach boldly and prophesy courageously.

Which was the real Jeremiah? In a sense, both of them—but the old needed to give way to the new, because the new was the way God had created him to be.

God is calling you to do the new you. The new you is who you really are, you just haven't seen the fullest expression of it yet because it's a lifelong process of self-discovery.

Ask yourself: *What does God know about me that I don't know about myself? What does God see in me that I've overlooked or even denied? Are there ways in which God has chosen me, but I still need to choose myself?*

> Are there ways in which God has chosen me, but I still need to choose myself?

You have a version of yourself in your mind, but it might not be the vision God has for you. If today's version of you doesn't match God's vision for you, it's time to come up higher. It's time to learn how he sees you and who he created you to be.

Nobody else can be that person: only you. That's why comparison is such a trap. You aren't trying to become like anyone else. Why would you sell yourself short like that? Strive to become like *you* instead.

The next time the old self tries to hold you back, remember the you God already knew. He has always known who you really are, so you can become all you were created to be. There is no shame in that, only endless possibility.

God doesn't see you as addicted or trapped or broken; he sees you as free, and he's with you in the fight. He sees that you struggle with those habits that feel like chains, but he also sees the strength in you by his Spirit to break those chains. He sees a version of you that is able to rise above feelings, a version that walks in faith even in the midst of uncertainty. It's a version that might seem unfamiliar and uncomfortable at first, but it's you.

Imagine yourself free. God knows *that* you.

Imagine yourself whole. God knows *that* you.

Imagine yourself overcoming habits that sabotage you. God knows *that* you.

Imagine yourself able to be patient and self-controlled, not giving in to every feeling that passes through your central nervous system. God knows *that* you.

Now, I'm not saying you can be or do anything you imagine. God doesn't always give you exactly what you pictured in life. If you're 5'4" and forty-seven years old, you're probably not going to play in the NBA. I think that is a healthy limitation to embrace. Your family will be happier and you'll put food on the table by acknowledging who you are not and choosing a different career path.

But I can tell you with confidence there is more to who you are than what you've experienced up until now, and God wants to give it to you.

You have to opt into the process, though. You have to choose to do the *new* you.

GRACE AND GRIT

In the coming pages, I want you to see yourself the way God sees you and to believe that you can make that vision your reality. As you walk it out, it will become natural. You'll find yourself saying, "I guess I *am* a patient person. I *am* a kind person. I *am* a good parent. I didn't used to feel that way, but I'm seeing it more and more now. I don't always act like it, but that's who I am, and I want to become more of it. And by God's grace, I can."

Stop saying, "This is who I am, so get used to it," and instead say, "This is who I am *so far*, but I'm not dead yet, so God's not done yet. I'm still growing. I'm still changing. I'm still learning. I like a lot of things about this edition of me, but I don't like all of them, and I'm not stopping until I become who God says I can be!"

Doing the new you is always more about God's grace than your grit. That's why God says that *he* who began a good work in *you* will bring it to completion until the day of Christ Jesus (Philippians 1:6). He tells *you* to work out *your* salvation because *he* is at work in *you* to will and to act in order to fulfill *his* good purpose (Philippians 2:13). And he says that by *his* grace, *you* are what *you* are, and *his* grace is not without effect (1 Corinthians 15:10).

> Doing the new you is always more about God's grace than your grit.

He . . . you . . . he . . . you . . . he . . . you. Do you see the partnership? The teamwork? God creates, defines, and empowers, and you and I live it out.

As you are growing, as you are changing, God always has grace for you. Grace is God's patience with you and his power in you. Thank God for grace!

Let me be clear, though. Grace is patience *and* power. Grace is never an excuse to be lazy or a way to avoid change. That's the polar opposite of what I'm saying. Sometimes you hear people use grace as a cover-up for consistent, hurtful behavior. "I'm just a sinner saved by grace," they say, as if grace means they never need to change.

No, grace is the very means by which God changes us into the people he knows we can be. It comes from him but it flows through us. It's a work that happens in unison, and it happens over time.

So, when you have an outburst of anger, or when you reach for the pills, or when you manipulate and lie to get your way, or when you watch porn until three in the morning and can't connect in real life, or when you hold on to a grudge until it corrodes you from the inside—remember that's not who God is, so it can't be who you really are, and his power is at work in you to change.

God knows you are capable of kindness even if you struggle with your temper. He knows you were created to be generous even if you've settled into a pattern of hoarding what you have. He sees you as honest, patient, wise, faithful, loving, stable, and kind. That's who Jesus is, and Jesus is in you, so that's the real you, the new you. That's the you that you can choose.

GET THE RIGHT VOICE IN YOUR HEAD

Now, it may take a while for the version of you that God knew all along to become the version of you that you know in your everyday life. And to be honest, in some ways you'll always struggle with the switch.

I know I do. I'm not writing this book because of my victories. I'm writing because of my struggles and my belief in a God who gives victory incrementally. I'm writing this to you as a man who is determined to step more fully into his role as a parent, as a pastor, and simply as a person loved and known by God.

I'm not the person I want to be. Not by a long shot. I can preach on Sunday about God's never-ending grace for our mistakes and talk about how his strength is made perfect in our weakness, but Monday morning I can find myself deep in a funk, feeling like I failed, because I replay the mental tape of what I said in the pulpit and I think it's not good enough, so *I* must not be good enough. I can find myself snapping at the people that I love because my emotions are burned out. And instead of replenishing myself in healthy ways, I numb or scroll to the point that I feel like a zombie.

Sometimes I'm glad to be me, sometimes I'm proud to be me, and sometimes I'm embarrassed and scared to be me. But "me" is all I've got. And you know what? It's who God wants.

I'm not who I want to be yet, but I'm not giving up either. I'm determined to keep revamping and remodeling my inner self by the power of the Holy Spirit as I grow into the image of Christ in me. It's a choice. I have to constantly decide to be the more mature, more self-aware version of me, even when my moods are volatile and my emotions run high.

Ephesians 4 makes it sound so simple: just put off the old self and put on the new. The imagery here is like a change of clothing. It's like coming home, taking off your button-down and putting on your favorite hoodie.

If only it were that simple! I wish putting *off* the old self were as easy as slipping out of a suit. But it's not. It feels more like struggling out of a straitjacket. Old habits die hard, after all. And I wish putting *on* the new self were as simple as throwing on a sweatshirt. But it's not. You have to work at it.

You have to embrace the process.

The point is constant progress, not instant perfection. Perfection is an illusion anyway. Real transformation comes by making countless small, right choices that align with who you are in Christ, rather than making small, wrong choices that align with who you used to be.

Doing the new you means reframing and retraining your mind to react differently. After all, you might be new, but the world you live in is the same one it's always been, and the neural pathways that have developed from your habits are deeply grooved. That means you need mental models and philosophies that are aligned with God's Word, not with your past experiences or current circumstances. It means you're going to have to practice too.

That's why I want to walk with you into this new you, almost like a coach would do.

That's where the six mindsets come in. You can preach these six things to yourself wherever you go. Whether you're walking into a job interview, waiting for a medical report, pulling an all-nighter to study for finals, or just trying to get the kids through the Chick-fil-A drive-through, what you say to yourself matters a whole lot more than you might think because it has the power to change you from the inside out. No matter how people have labeled you or how you've labeled yourself in the past, if you get new language to define your-self and to describe who you are in Christ, you're going to be shocked at the person you become six weeks from now, six months from now, six years from now.

Each of these truths is very personal to me. These are the things I repeat to myself when I'm going to preach on Sunday morning, or when I'm trying to get my act together as a parent, or when I'm just pulling myself out of bed on a Monday morning. I preach these things, I pray these things, I say these things, and I believe these things for you and for me.

With each of these mindsets, there is a call to action that God will enable you to take. It's one thing to say you are changed, forgiven, and redeemed, but it's another thing to *be* that in your daily life.

I'm going to share the whole list with you now, just to give you a preview before we move forward.

1. *I'm not stuck unless I stop.*
   Action Step: Commit to progress.

2. *Christ is in me. I am enough.*
   Action Step: Accept your Self.

3. *With God there's always a way, and by faith I will find it.*
   Action Step: Focus on possibility.

4. *God is not against me, but he's in it with me, working through me, fighting for me.*
   Action Step: Walk in confidence.

5. *My joy is my job.*
   Action Step: Own your emotions.

6. *God has given me everything I need for the season I'm in.*
   Action Step: Embrace your now.

I'm getting fired up just listing these declarations! I hope you are too. In fact, if you can, say a few of them out loud right now. See how they feel coming out of your mouth. I want you to get a good sense of what God is speaking over you so you can step into it with expectation. As you incorporate these things into your belief system, you'll begin to act and talk in new ways.

I know these six statements are simple, and that's on purpose. They are meant to be easy to memorize, like a song or a slogan would be. In fact, I have written songs based on some of these. I want them to be like tracks on repeat in your heart so your faith can work in real life.

God's power at work in you gives you the freedom to do the new you. As long as you have breath in your lungs, you are not locked into the current version of you. You have autonomy. You have options. You have the power to get out of traps, off of treadmills, and into truth.

You'll never be more loved than you are right now. You'll never be more accepted than you are this instant. The work of Jesus settled that once and for all. You don't need to stress and strive to somehow prove yourself to God.

Stop before you even read the next sentence and celebrate how far God has already brought you, how many obstacles you've overcome, how many paths he's already opened for you, and how many amazing things he's done through you.

If you think you have to fix yourself in order to get God to love you more, you're starting from the wrong assumption. *You'll never be more loved than you are right now.* You'll never be more accepted than you are this instant. The work of Jesus settled that once and for all. You don't need to stress and strive to somehow prove yourself to God.

God is close to you, and he blesses you, and he is proud of you, and he is cheering you on *right now*. He's not just barely tolerating the present-day you because he's holding out hope that someday you'll be worthy.

Every version of you is still you. It's all intentional. It's all working together to serve a big-picture purpose. Even those things that haven't worked out yet are going to fit into the plan God has for your future.

You are the one God loves. That needs to be your starting point. But where you start isn't where you have to stay. That's why I'm so excited about these six mindsets. When you choose to think and live in these ways, you are choosing *you*. You are deciding to overcome distraction, defeat, and discouragement so you can press into all God created you to be.

> His calling is your confidence, and his grace is your guarantee.

I know this to be true: wherever you are in your journey, God has good things planned for you. I'm not saying you won't face challenges or make mistakes along the way, but I believe God sees good days ahead for you. He has prepared good works for you to do. His calling is your confidence, and his grace is your guarantee.

The *knew* you and the *new* you are the same you, and they are the right you. They're the best version of you because they're God's version of you, and by faith you can step into what God already sees.

The first mindset we're going to look at is the foundation for all the rest: *You aren't stuck unless you stop.* Why does this matter so much? Because without a commitment to progress, you're defeated before you start. But if you can get deep into your heart and mind that you serve an unstoppable God who is leading you forward, no distraction, deception, difficulty, or devil can stand in your way.

MINDSET (01)

I'M NOT STUCK UNLESS I STOP.

ACTION STEP:
COMMIT TO PROGRESS.

TWO

IT'S NOT THAT SIMPLE

Recently I was at a wrestling match watching my son Graham. A lady behind us was cheering at the top of her lungs for her team, the Spiders. The Spiders were not doing well. This particular match was in the heavyweight division, which goes up to 285 pounds. The boy who was winning was every bit of those 285 pounds, and the Spider trapped underneath him was not. No matter how hard he tried, the kid couldn't move.

From behind me I heard the lady yelling, "Get up! Get up! Stand up!"

The kid couldn't hear her, of course, but if he could have, I can only imagine his response. "Oh, yeah! I forgot! That's what I'm supposed to do—*stand up*. Thank you, lady at the top of the bleachers, for reminding me what I'm supposed to be doing here. It's easy. It's obvious. Just stand up."

But we all know it's not that simple.

When you're stuck, the last thing you need are condescending voices from the nosebleeds telling you to do the

27

thing you already wish you were doing, the thing you're trying with all your might to do, the thing that's so easy to advise
from the comfort of someone else's life.

You want to tell them, "Yeah, why don't you try it? Why
don't you get down here on the mat? Why don't you try dealing with my boss's impossible demands? Why don't you try
being a single parent juggling two jobs and three kids? Why
don't you try paying off school loans while making a rent
payment every month? Why don't you try recovering from
the loss of a loved one? You don't know my life, so don't tell
me why it's so easy."

When you're stuck in a rut, in a habit, in a creative slump,
in a dead-end job, in an addiction, in a toxic relationship, in
an illness, in anxiety, in a bad mood, in depression, in debt,
in discouragement—what you *don't* need are shame and
blame. You don't need someone yelling at you to just get up
and get over it. What you need is someone who understands
your situation to be with you in the middle of it. Someone to
encourage you through it. Someone to help you carry it.

That's exactly what God does.

God doesn't just yell at you from heaven, "Get up! Stand
up! Do more! Fight harder! Sin less! Stop doubting! Be better!" He doesn't shame you for being stuck, because he knows
what you're going through. The Bible says, "For we do not
have a high priest who is unable to empathize with our weaknesses, but we have one who has been tempted in every way,
just as we are—yet he did not sin. Let us then approach God's
throne of grace with confidence, so that we may receive mercy
and find grace to help us in our time of need" (Hebrews
4:15–16).

Instead of yelling at you from the stands, God jumps into the battle with you. Life isn't a high-school wrestling match, after all, and you don't have to fight alone. In your time of need, his mercy is there for you. His grace is with you. His strength is in you.

> Instead of yelling at you from the stands, God jumps into the battle with you.

I know that can be hard to believe if your child is in the hospital, or if your car breaks down and the mechanic says it will cost two thousand dollars to fix it, or if you just found out your husband is cheating on you. When you are crushed and suffocated by the weight of opposition, giving up can feel like the only option.

But it's not.

That is what I want you to get deep into your heart and your mind: you're not stuck unless you stop, and you don't have to stop because God is with you in the fight.

When facing difficult circumstances, the old way of doing you might have said, "I'm stuck. That's why I stopped. That's why I quit praying. That's why I quit trying. That's why I gave into cynicism. That's why I quit taking care of my body. That's why I started medicating with alcohol. That's why I'm such a bitter person. In fact, I'm not bitter, I'm just realistic: I'm trapped. I tried all the church stuff, the religion stuff, the God stuff, but it didn't work. I tried being kind, but people used my niceness as an opportunity to take advantage of me, so I stopped being the bigger person."

That was the old you and the old me. That version of ourselves saw *stuck* as a reason to *stop*. It was a mentality that relied only on you and always on you: your strength, your resources, your experience, your intelligence. When the old you was pinned underneath a 285-pound challenge, it gave up. It tapped out. What else could you do?

But the new you knows a different truth. The new you embraces the mindset "I'm not stuck unless I stop."

This version of you does not live in denial, but it doesn't surrender to disappointment either. It doesn't give up easily. It doesn't hide from challenges. Instead of avoiding life's giants, it attacks them with confidence in God. The new you does whatever is needed for as long as it takes until you regain your momentum and can move forward again.

The new you is aware of problems but committed to progress. That means asking for help if needed. It means opening yourself up to new ideas and greater creativity. It means getting advice from people who have been where you are before.

> The new you is aware of problems but committed to progress.

Several years ago I realized I needed to learn more about managing my money and long-term planning. My dad had taught me everything he knew about finances, but I didn't understand the different types of investments the way I needed to, and I knew it. I felt trapped. I felt frustrated. The fear of risk and loss seemed to be greater than the reward of learning and growing.

Then I remembered a friend of mine who is ten years ahead of where I am financially who had offered several times to help me with financial planning. I reached out and asked him for two hours of his time. We scheduled a phone call, and he gave me a list of the different categories of investments, along with the goals he's hit and the mistakes he's made along the way.

I remember feeling a sense of freedom after that call. I wasn't a master of money by any means, but at least I had a map. I could see a way forward.

It's funny how quickly you can go from exasperated to excited.

From agitated to animated.

From immovable to unstoppable.

All it takes is a glimpse of the next step.

See, stuck is a way of saying you can't move forward and *there's nothing you can do about it.* Circumstances have assumed control. Things are hopeless and you are helpless, so you might as well quit trying. It's a frustrating, powerless feeling.

But that's not how God operates. That's not even his nature. He's not a frustrated, powerless God, and he didn't create you to live a frustrated, powerless life.

God is the waymaker. He is all-powerful, all-knowing, all-consuming. He causes valleys to be raised up and mountains be made low. He turns graves into gardens and bones into armies. Our God is a sea-splitting, stone-rolling, wind-whispering, fire-from-heaven, water-from-the-rock, stop-the-moon-in-the-sky kind of God.

When you feel hopeless, he is nearer than ever. As an old country preacher said, "When you're down to nothing, God is up to something!" In those moments when your story seems stuck and hope is lost, God will make a way for you. He wants to give you back your courage, your power, your expectation.

That phone call about financial advice is just one example. I could list a hundred times I've said I was stuck, but I wasn't—I had just stopped. I had stopped thinking about the problem creatively and started self-sabotaging and withdrawing into isolation out of fear. I had stopped praying and asking God to show me my next step. I had stopped strategizing with the mind of the Spirit, and I was walking only in the limitation of my own experience.

Now don't get me wrong, this isn't a name-it-and-claim-it approach to faith. I'm not saying that obstacles are all in your head or that every problem you face can be prayed away overnight. I realize some situations and variables are outside of your control. I also realize that change doesn't happen in a moment, and some states of mind require a long time to be rewired by the Holy Spirit. And of course, in certain situations you might need to seek professional help or advice.

You can expect to put work into moving forward. You should plan on knocking on a lot of doors and asking for a lot of help. Jesus said, "Ask and it will be given to you; seek and you will find; knock and the door will be opened to you. For everyone who asks receives; the one who seeks finds; and to the one who knocks, the door will be opened" (Matthew 7:7–8). There's no shame in asking, seeking, and knocking. It doesn't mean you lack faith, and it doesn't mean God fell asleep on the job.

It just means you're putting in the work to get to where you need to be.

But if you don't believe you can move forward, you won't ask or seek or knock. You'll just sit there, miserable under 285 pounds of weight, wishing you were somewhere else while people in the nosebleeds holler at you.

Now, keep in mind that the way forward might not be what you thought it would be. God's idea of progress and his definition of success don't always make sense to us at first. Sometimes we get so caught up in our expectations of what we think is supposed to happen that we don't recognize the doors God is opening right in front of us. How often do we miss an opportunity because our idea of what should happen is too narrow? Too small? Too human?

Maybe God didn't heal you, but that doesn't mean he abandoned you. It doesn't mean your faith failed. He is doing other things in you and through you. His grace is sufficient for you.

Maybe you got fired from that job, but that doesn't mean your life is over. God has something else ahead, but you might have to pivot. You might have to cast your net on the other side.

Don't give the obstacle, the enemy, the failure too much credit. No matter what has made you feel stuck, God is bigger than that thing, and he's already on the other side of it. It's not the end of the road. It's just a curve you can't see past. Maybe it's even a fork that will open up new opportunities. If you give up now, you'll never know what miracle God has just ahead.

Say it to yourself: "I'm not stuck unless I stop. I might be temporarily incapacitated. I might be facing something I've never faced before, something that seems too big for me. I might have to rethink, recalibrate, reset. But God is on my side. I can go to his throne of grace in this time of need. God is bigger than my battle. He's

> If you give up now, you'll never know what miracle God has just ahead.

sovereign in this situation. He's greater than my circumstance, so it's only a matter of time before I find the way forward."

That might not be how the old you treated obstacles, but you're not doing the old you anymore. You're doing the new you. You're stepping into the you God sees, and that version of you is committed to progress.

THREE

DON'T ARGUE FOR YOUR LIMITATIONS

My dad grew up in a really rough household. His own dad, my grandfather, was an alcoholic, a mean drunk who physically abused his family. Then, on my dad's seventh or eighth birthday, my grandfather died by suicide. Those things deeply affected my dad. He determined he was going to break the cycle with his own kids. It was important to my parents to give us opportunities and to enable us to go forward.

I remember when I was in high school, somebody told my dad I would never be able to afford college. My dad never even graduated from high school, so that triggered him. He shut the person down. "Don't say that! Don't ever tell my boy he can't go to college. I'll rob a bank if I have to. I'll kill somebody and take their money to pay for him if he wants to go to college."

I'm not saying that's ethical, but it meant a lot to me. It sent me a message. "Don't let my limitations become your insecurities. It might be my history, but it's not my legacy. You can do something different."

That's a message we need to tell ourselves on a regular basis. I'm not saying we should go around threatening to rob banks and kill people, but when it comes to breaking cycles that hold us back, a certain level of aggression is appropriate.

Instead of that, though, I sometimes find myself doing the opposite. I excuse my limitations. I defend them.

Why? Well, when I think about it, there are a couple of reasons. First, I feel loyal to some of my limitations because they've been "me" for so long. They are so deeply ingrained in me that I think they *are* me.

Second, it can feel brutally vulnerable to make changes, to take risks, to put myself out there, to accept responsibility, to pursue a dream. And vulnerability is not exactly hardwired into humans. In the face of risk, we often choose retreat. In the name of self-protection, we often self-sabotage. Limiting ourselves feels safer than believing in ourselves, so we fabricate arguments to "prove" why we can't do the very things God has created us to do and empowered us to do.

Do you ever do this? Maybe you know something needs to change, you know God is calling you higher, but you let *loyalty* to a past version of you or *fear* of doing something you've never done before get in your way. A mindset that says "I'm not stuck unless I stop" is a mindset that refuses to let either of these things hold you back from living up to your calling and abilities.

I once heard a motivational speaker named Les Brown say, "If you argue for your limitations you get to keep them." It's tragic but true. How many times in my life have I been more loyal to my limitations than I was to my potential? How often am I a defense attorney for the things that hold me back, even when God is trying to move me forward?

Do you ever argue for your limitations so effectively that you end up keeping them? Do you ever defend your limited definition of who you are to a God who has known you longer than you have and who sees you with more faith and grace than you do?

Maybe you have a great business idea, but you won't even take the first steps to see if it's viable because you've already talked yourself out of it. *I'll probably fail. I'm not smart enough. This is a stupid idea. People are just going to laugh.* You're so scared that you won't be able to do it that you write yourself off before you even try.

I've written myself off more times than I care to admit, and maybe you have too. Maybe you dismiss a character issue by saying, "That's just my personality." You excuse a parenting fail by saying, "I didn't have a good example of that growing up." You excuse a bad decision at work by saying, "I'm too busy, too overwhelmed, too stressed, too stupid, so that's just the best I can do."

God sends you signs and signals that there is more in you. He shows you things you can do and places he wants to take you. But if you respond with, "I could never do that; I'll never be that," if you argue for your limitations, you get to keep them. You get to live with them.

In Ephesians 4, just before Paul said to put off the old self, he wrote, "That, however, is not the way of life you learned when you heard about Christ and were taught in him in accordance with the truth that is in Jesus" (verses 20–21). The "way of life" Paul described was one of impurity, indulgence, loss of sensitivity, ignorance, and hardness of heart. That was what his readers had always known and heard.

I can imagine them saying, "But, Paul, that's the way my dad did it. That's the way my mom did it. That's what I've always heard. That's what I've always thought. That's what so-and-so said. That's just how we do it. That's just how I am. I'm just doing me."

Paul confronts their loyalty to a past way of thinking by saying, "Guys, you were taught wrong. That might be who you thought you were, but it's just the layers of lifestyle that have accumulated from the things you learned. There's a new you created in God before the foundation of the world. You need to relearn how to do you."

The old way of living is the patterns and learned behaviors of the past. It takes intentionality and commitment to unlearn the old way you were taught and learn a new way. That means you have to pay attention to what you're saying about yourself and why you assume it's true.

If you tell yourself, "They put me in a bad mood," then you get to keep your bad mood. If you say, "I have a short temper; that's who I am," then you get to keep your anger. But if you're burning through perfectly good relationships and hurting the people you love because you get moody or fly off the handle too quickly, why defend that? Why be loyal to that version of you?

Or maybe you never learned to apologize. It always felt like weakness. It felt like humiliation. But now you're learning that you don't have to defend yourself all the time. You can trust God to be the one who justifies you, the one who gives you value and security. That's not what you were taught, though. That's not what you saw in the home you grew up in. So at first it feels unnatural to say, "I'm sorry. I was wrong. I'll do better."

When you are being called by God to change, it can feel like a betrayal of what you've always been, and that brings up all kinds of emotions. "Oh, no! If I stop being controlling, how am I going to deal with stress? If I stop being manipulative, things will fall apart. I won't get what I want. I won't get what I need. People are going to take advantage of me."

But those arguments don't protect you. They limit you. They feel comfortable because they're familiar, but they're not your friends. They're not moving you forward. And they don't deserve your loyalty.

God is teaching you a new way of life, and that means you can't be loyal to your limitations. You can't make a case for the things in you that are not like Christ. I'm not saying to ignore your limitations, but a lot of us go far beyond acknowledging our limitations. We actually become advocates for them.

When the devil tells you that you're worthless, do you start collecting evidence to help him? Do you say, "That's right, I *am* worthless," and then list all the evidence from your past that backs up that accusation? Do you go out and do things that make you feel even more worthless?

When you feel too old to try something new, do you agree with that feeling? "I'm too old to do this or to learn that. It's too late. You can't teach an old dog new tricks." If you argue for your limitation, you can feel old at age forty. I met a twenty-year-old the other day who told me, "Man, I'm getting old." Really, bro? At twenty? Just wait. You have no idea. At least that's what one of my mentors who just turned seventy tells me.

I think we need to add another sentence to that motivational phrase. "If you argue for your limitations, you get to keep them. *But if you agree with God about your potential, you get to grow into it."*

What potential? The potential God sees in you. The doors he is opening for you. The gifts and calling he is drawing out of you. If God says you can change, you can change. If he says you can help somebody, you can help somebody. If he says he put something in you, then he can call it out of you.

> If you argue for your limitations, you get to keep them. *But if you agree with God about your potential, you get to grow into it.*

Is your limitation shouting louder than your potential? Because you won't *move* past it until you can *see* past it. You'll settle for the status quo. You'll argue for your limitations. You'll advocate for the very things that hold you back because you can't visualize a future where you are free from them.

You have to catch a vision of the version of you that God sees, because that vision will pull you out of what you're stuck in and propel you toward what you were created for. Once you agree with God about what he sees in you and what he says about you, you'll stop fighting your future.

As I mentioned already, fear of failure is one of the biggest motivations behind our arguments. We often defend our status quo because we're afraid that if we try to change it, we'll fail—and failure seems like a worse outcome than staying stuck.

I remember a stand-up comic who was talking about learning to perform in public, and he said something to the effect of, "You've got to bomb in order to get good. You've just gotta get up, bomb in front of an audience, then realize,

Oh, that happened, and I didn't die. Nobody hunted me down and killed me for it. They moved on and forgot about it."

That sounds a little depressing, but it's actually encouraging. Fear of failure can be such a loud voice in your head that you never attempt to take that next step. In the moment you face the thing you fear, though, God strengthens you for it. You have to be willing to put yourself out there and do the thing you believe God is calling you to do, even if it bombs once or twice. Then you realize, "Oh, that wasn't so bad. In all of these areas I was freaking out about, God was already at work. I can do this. I can get there. I can be that person I see ahead. I can overcome the obstacle I'm facing. I've got some work to do, but I can't imagine going back to the old me now."

You have to listen to God's arguments *for* you or you'll be persuaded by your own arguments *against* you every time. You'll let the devil's lies and the world's labels define you. They can't see the real you, though. Only God can do that, but you have to agree with him.

Remember the twelve spies Moses sent into the Promised Land? They came back saying, "We seemed like grasshoppers in our own eyes, and we looked the same to them" (Numbers 13:33). They argued for a grasshopper self-image, and they lived a grasshopper existence in the wilderness for the next forty years.

The following generation had a different mindset, though. At some point, they rejected the way their parents thought about themselves and God. That doesn't mean they were disrespectful, but they drew lines. They learned. They grew. And when Joshua sent two spies to check out the land, they came back with an optimistic report: "The LORD has surely given the whole land into our hands; all the people are melting in fear because of us" (Joshua 2:24).

The new generation looked at the same land, the same enemies, the same risks—but they had a different mentality. They agreed with God about their potential, and that set them up for growth and victory.

The old version of you got you this far, so don't hate it. Just don't defend it when it comes time to change. Your past failures and successes are all part of who you are, but they don't get to decide who you will become.

Agree with God and commit to progress. Say, "All right, God. I don't know if I see myself this way, but you do. You think I have what it takes, and that's why you let me face this situation. You obviously know something about me that I don't, so I'm going to step up. I'm going to rise to the level of your expectations, not sink to the level of my experience."

> Your past failures and successes are all part of who you are, but they don't get to decide who you will become.

Ask yourself: Am I arguing for my limitations or my potential? Am I defending what I've always done or developing what God says I can do? Am I agreeing with my fear or with my future?

It's a choice you make. It's a mindset you put on. You're not stuck unless you stop, so agree with God and grow into your potential.

FOUR

DEFY YOUR DEFAULT

About ten years ago, I started to notice that none of my pants fit anymore. They weren't shrinking—I was growing. For a while, I wore joggers every day in denial of the reality of my expanding waistline, but I finally ended up paying a tailor to let out my pants. I don't think that's what the prayer of Jabez means when it says "enlarge my territory."

I remember looking at the tailor and saying, "I hate this! I could be using this money for a lot of other things. Instead, I'm paying you to make my clothes bigger."

He said, "Keep eating! It's job security for me."

Eventually something clicked inside of me, though, and I began to redefine my relationship with exercise. Up to that point, I was an on-again, off-again exerciser who was usually on some form of low-carb diet, or at least trying to be. But I would always tell people, "I hate exercise. I don't like to work out. I don't like to lift weights. I did back in high school, but I don't really like going to the gym now. I don't do CrossFit. I definitely don't do cardio or leg day. If you do, that's great, but that's not me."

That was my default.

Until I decided to defy my default. To change what had become second nature to me by the power of habit. I began to consistently do the thing that would make me the me I had the potential to be, at least physically.

I turned a room in my house into a workout space. I started with just a bench, some adjustable Bowflex dumbbells, and a treadmill somebody gave me. I took a little Bluetooth speaker into the room because I figured lifting weights would be less painful with Led Zeppelin in the background. I got several of my friends to agree to come over and work out with me four days a week.

I even named the workout room. I called it the POUND. It's an acronym: The Place of Ultimate Natural Development. I know, it's epic. Sometimes it takes epic (and a little bit corny) to get you motivated every day to do something you don't want to do.

I told my workout partners, "Guys, I'm not an exercise person, so I'm not doing chin-ups. I'm not doing burpees. I'm not doing squats." I set the bar low because I wasn't sure I was actually going to change.

To motivate myself a little, I hung a chart on the wall, and every time I worked out, I put a star on it because I thought that would reinforce the behavior. It did, even though I felt a little silly. I was a grown man with a beard putting stars on a chart like a seven-year-old.

That was over ten years ago. Not long ago I added up all the star charts from over the years, and I was surprised to see

I had worked out over two thousand times in ten years. And yet, just the other day, I was talking to somebody about exercise, and I caught myself saying, "You know, I'm not necessarily a workout person . . ."

Then I stopped myself. I realized that yes, actually, I *am* "a workout person."

I didn't used to be. I didn't think I was. I never saw myself that way before. But now I am someone who loves working out and who does it consistently. Why would I deny it? Why would I downplay it? It's something I enjoy, it's a good example for my kids, and it's healthy.

I'm not saying this to brag. I'm not trying to sell you protein powder or a gym membership. I'm just saying it to make the point that I still believed I wasn't that kind of person even after all the work I had put in. I was stuck in an old way of seeing myself: someone who wasn't strong, wasn't consistent, wasn't committed in this area of my life. Even after two thousand stars on the chart.

I was a workout person. I just wasn't aware of it.

When did the switch happen? When did I become an "exercise guy"? Was it workout #522? Workout #1396? We all know it doesn't work like that. There wasn't one workout where I became that kind of person.

But somewhere along the way, star by star, the old version of me became a newer version of me. The weaker version became a stronger version. And I like this version better.

We don't always know who we are, even as we are becoming it. We don't know what we'll enjoy, what we could be good at, or what we could grow into.

But God does.

In order to step into that new you, you have to challenge the old you.

That's where the mindset "I'm not stuck unless I stop" takes on a deeper, more personal meaning. It doesn't just apply to overcoming obstacles and getting around roadblocks you face as you go through your day. It also applies to the ongoing process of *inner* growth, of becoming who God made you to be and stepping into the calling he placed upon you.

When God called Joshua to lead Israel, he knew Joshua needed to see himself differently than he had up until that point. I think Joshua was struggling with some self-doubt. He had just taken over from Moses, the guy who led Israel out of Egypt, so he had big sandals to fill. And he was supposed to lead Israel into the Promised Land, which was an impossible goal unless God did a whole lot of miracles.

Joshua knew all that, and God knew Joshua knew all that. So God challenged him to confront his old way of seeing himself. God promised him, "No one will be able to stand against you all the days of your life. As I was with Moses, so I will be with you; I will never leave you nor forsake you. Be strong and courageous, because you will lead these people to inherit the land I swore to their ancestors to give them" (Joshua 1:5–6).

Joshua's default seems to have been fear and insecurity. His default was to be second-in-command. But it was time to challenge those default settings and step into the new Joshua, a Joshua who wasn't new at all, because it was the Joshua God had known since the beginning of time.

What does God see in you that you can't see in yourself? What defaults do you need to defy? Where have you been stuck so long that you've assumed this is who you really are and who you'll always be? Only you can know where you have settled for a "normal" that isn't meant to be normal at all because it isn't the new you.

Maybe when you argue with your spouse, your default is to get angry and storm out of the room, followed by the silent treatment. Maybe when you're around other people, your default is self-doubt or conflict avoidance, so you don't speak up when you know you should. Maybe your default is suspicion, so you have a hard time trusting people or building good friendships. Maybe your default is stinginess and none of your employees are happy because they feel used by you.

One of my defaults that I've had to work on is how I take criticism. I remember many years ago, after I went on a mission trip in China, my leader told me, "Steven, your biggest problem is that you're defensive."

I responded, "No, I'm not!"

Ironic, isn't it? If I defend my defensiveness, I've proven the point of my accuser.

But I don't have to do that. I can defy my own defensiveness. I can choose to listen. I can take some space and time to consider the criticism instead of punching back. I can say, "Let me think about that. Let me get back to you." I can ask God if there is real value in what that person is saying even if I don't agree with it. I don't have to defend myself because I don't depend on someone else's opinion to define me anyway.

> As I incorporate the confidence of Christ in my life, I begin to defy my default, and I grow into something I never knew I could be.

Do you see how this works? As I incorporate the confidence of Christ in my life, I begin to defy my default, and I grow into something I never knew I could be. God knew it was there, though. He's calling it out of me, and he's calling me into it.

It takes self-awareness. It takes work. It takes courage and humility. And most of all, it takes time.

But somewhere along the way, you become "that person." That patient person. That kind person. That relaxed person. That pure person. The person God saw in you even when you never saw it in yourself.

Was it kind word #522 that did it? Was it good decision #1396? No, of course not. It doesn't work like that with your maturity any more than it does with your muscles.

But it does work. You do change. The Bible says we "are being transformed into his image with ever-increasing glory, which comes from the Lord, who is the Spirit" (2 Corinthians 3:18). It's a process, and God's in charge. Let him set the pace.

As you pursue the new you, you'll have to defy your default time and time again. You'll find yourself caught between your comfort and your calling; between what you've always done and what God is inviting you to do next.

I mentioned earlier that this can feel unnatural at first, but that doesn't make it wrong. I remember trying to learn how to play tennis, and the first thing the instructor told me was, "Show me how you hold your racket." I showed him, and immediately he moved my hand to a completely different position. For the next few weeks, I felt like a four-year-old every time I served. The ball was flying everywhere. In order for my serve to come up to a higher standard, I had to switch my grip, and it felt terrible. But gradually it got better. Now, I'm not challenging Novak Djokovic anytime soon, but I did improve.

At first, though, I got worse.

That's the thing about defying your default. When you first try, it feels unnatural, awkward, difficult. That can be embarrassing—if you let it be. If you expect immediate perfection, you might be tempted to give up because the learning process exposes how much you don't know and how far you still have to go. But with the Holy Spirit as your instructor and guide, growth isn't just possible. It's inevitable. As long as you don't give up too soon.

Are there areas of your character, your attitude, or your actions where you need to defy your default, even if it feels a little awkward at first? Are there circumstances in your life you've accepted as normal that you need to fight to change, even though there is some resistance? Is God calling you, like Joshua, to step into a new role that is a little intimidating?

Wherever you are in God's process, no matter how old you are or how long you've been doing things this way, and regardless of how uncomfortable the "new you" feels at first, don't stop changing. Don't quit growing.

> Your default is not your destiny.

Your default is not your destiny. It's just where you are today and it's how you act right now. But you are growing. You are changing. The struggle itself is your Place Of Ultimate (Super)natural Development. You're not working out your abs; you're working out your salvation. You're living out your identity, and you're being transformed into the image of God through Jesus.

As long as you don't stop, as long as you don't settle, as long as you don't make excuses for a version of yourself that is beneath the one God knew before the beginning of time, your default can't define or deter you.

It's just a starting point, and you are being transformed more and more each day into the image of God in you.

FIVE

DO THE THING THAT YOU WOULD DO

When I was twelve years old, I wanted so badly to be in a rock band. I dreamed about it. I obsessed over it. I fantasized about it. The problem was that I didn't really play any instruments and neither did any of my friends.

So I created imaginary bands. I would make up a cool-sounding band name, then I would go to a friend and say, "Yo, man, you're in my band. You're my drummer."

And he would say, "What are you talking about? I don't play the drums. I've never taken a lesson in my life. I don't even have a drum set."

"It doesn't matter. You're the drummer in my band." Then I'd go find a bass player who didn't play bass, a lead singer who couldn't sing, and so on. I would even create fictional CDs for my imaginary bands.

Eventually, a friend of mine named Michelle told me about a guy who played bass. By that time I was getting better at the guitar, but I still didn't have any friends who could be in a band. So I asked her, "Does he really play bass?"

She said, "Yes."

I said, "Does he own a bass?"

"Yeah."

"I want to meet him."

We started a band together. He went by the name Fox, which was his middle name. Eventually his brother James joined too, and now we had a legitimate three-piece band. We named our group Deadbeat. I was on guitar, Fox on bass, and James on drums. We would play Pearl Jam, Hootie & the Blowfish, Bush, and lots of Green Day. We'd perform anywhere anybody asked us to go. We didn't care. As long as they had enough electrical outlets for us to plug into, and as long as nobody would kick us out for making too much noise, we would play for them. I'm not saying we were on the verge of a record deal, but at least I was finally in a band.

Eventually James had to quit, so we got another drummer. Then he quit and we found another drummer. Eventually, the band fizzled, and here I am today, back to not having a band. That's okay. I still write songs and love rock music.

> Do the thing you would do if you knew God was making a way forward.

I laugh at twelve-year-old me now. How weird is it to start a fake band and put out fake albums? But it didn't feel weird to me at the time. I didn't have a real band, so I just did all the things that I would do if I *did* have a band until I actually had one. Fake it till you make it, right?

I think the story illustrates a simple principle that can help you in any area of your life. When you aren't where you want to be yet, do the thing that you *would* do if you were already there, or at least get as close as you can.

In other words, ask yourself what you *would* do if you didn't have the limitation, the obstacle, the giant standing in your path. Then do whatever you can to head in that direction, even if it's only a tiny step, and even if you don't know what you're going to do when you get there. Do the thing you would do if you knew God was making a way forward.

That's what commitment to progress is all about. That's how you get unstuck. That's why you never stop. Success doesn't come through superhuman feats of strength or by finding shortcuts nobody else knows about. Success is found in every step you take in the right direction.

Maybe you say, "If I had an hour free, I would exercise." But you don't have an hour—you only have ten minutes. Well, exercise for ten minutes. If exercise is the thing you would do if you had more time, do a mini version of that thing.

Maybe you say, "If I had enough money, I'd buy a house." What would you do if you did have enough for that down payment? You'd buy the house and start making payments. Why not start saving for the payments now? Holly and I opened a bank account for our first house and separated part of our paycheck to get ready for a mortgage payment before we even had the down payment. We wanted to set the pattern for the potential that we believed God had put inside of us.

Do the thing you would do. Don't wait. Do whatever you can, no matter how small, that moves you in the direction of the thing you would do if you could.

Don't say, "If I can't do it this way, I'm not going to do it at all." That's a recipe for staying stuck. Conditions will never be perfect. Your expectations will never be fully met. If you wait for everything to be easy and obvious and risk-free, you'll never go anywhere. Ecclesiastes 11:4 says, "Whoever watches the wind will not plant; whoever looks at the clouds will not reap." In other words, if you try hard enough, you can always talk yourself out of the next step of faith.

> Sometimes you just have to work with what you've got. You have to use what God has put in your hand, no matter how unlikely or limited it is.

Sometimes you just have to work with what you've got. You have to use what God has put in your hand, no matter how unlikely or limited it is. You do the thing that you would do, even if it's only a preview, a practice round for the real thing.

Now, this phrase "Do the thing that you would do" actually has a double meaning. To me, it doesn't just mean do the thing that you *would* do if you weren't facing the obstacle or limitation in front of you.

In light of Ephesians 4, it also means "Do the thing *that* you would do."

Which you? *That* you. The new you. The one God knew since creation. The new you he is calling you to step into now. *That* version of you is the right you, the true you. So when you're facing a tough choice or situation, do the thing that *that* you would do.

Do you want to be known as a generous person? Do the thing *that* you would do: the generous you. The loving you. The selfless you. You've seen glimpses of you in a generous state. Do more of the thing *that* version of you would do, and it'll turn from a glimpse into a grounded reality.

Are you dealing with a delay? Do the thing that the patient, proactive you would do. Take the steps you can take and leave the rest to God. Move in the flow of the Holy Spirit.

Don't force it in frustration, but don't just wait around either. Picture yourself as the person who moves forward in step with the Holy Spirit and do the thing *that* you would do.

Are you beginning to see how this works? How you see yourself matters. What you think you are capable of is crucial. Psychologists use terms like *self-efficacy* and *self-image* to refer to the same truth. Coming from a place of faith, we understand that we were made in the image of God. We are created to be like him. We get to defy our default. We don't have to lapse into what we've always done.

"Do the thing that you would do," therefore, is a strategy to break out of lethargy. It's a way to focus our faith during those moments where we feel conflicted. It's a challenge to come up higher. It's a summons to faith.

So spend time with God, get his vision of the you you're becoming, and start living like that person now. Don't act out of your old self, your old patterns. Act your way into your new self with the power of the Holy Spirit.

> We don't all do generosity or patience or love or joy the same way, so focus on figuring out what the real you would do, not what someone else would do.

What would *that* you do? The one you want to be. The one God called. The one God knows intimately. The one God is bringing you into in this moment. That you is not just an aspiration; it's authentic. That you *is* you, so start doing that you. And keep doing it, by faith, until you become this you in your behavior, until you find yourself living out your God-created potential.

Remember, too, that "that you" is not going to look the same as anybody else. Do the thing that *you* would do. We don't all do generosity or patience or love or joy the same way, so focus on figuring out what the real you would do, not what someone else would do.

I have friends who are gardeners, which requires a type of patience I don't even aspire to. But I am patient in other ways: in how I study and prepare for sermons, in how I nurture song ideas, in how I allow God to move people in and out of my life. I might not demonstrate my patience in planting and pruning tomatoes, but I do plant and prune truth in the hearts of people. Become the you God created and called *you* to be, not what he created and called someone else to be.

Notice also that when I said, "Do the thing that you would do," I intentionally didn't say, "Do *all the things* that you would do." I said, "the thing." Singular.

Doing "all the things" is overwhelming and unrealistic. Doing all the things will put you in a hospital bed, or at the very least give you insomnia or ulcers. It's a sure road to burnout. Pick one or two things that *that* you would do in your current situation and do those.

I heard an older minister say that his favorite scripture when he was young was "I can do *all* things through Christ who strengthens me." But now that he was older, his favorite scripture was "This *one* thing I do." He had learned the power of focus.

What is the thing God is calling you to focus on right now? Do that thing. One thing at a time. To fight for the new you means to focus on the next important priority that the Holy Spirit is pointing to in your life.

Would *that* you pray? Then prayer is the thing that you should do right now. Would *that* you show up on time to work? Then being on time is the thing that you should do.

Would *that* you tell the truth? Start a business? Turn off your phone and be present? Say you're sorry? Save for retirement? Stand up for somebody who can't stand up for themselves? Refuse to gossip? Choose love?

Then do that thing. And then the next thing. And then the next.

A few years ago, before my father passed away, he and I went through a really rough patch in our relationship. He had been diagnosed with ALS, and between his failing health and some medication he was taking that affected his moods, things were really difficult.

For the last two years of his life, in particular, he was impossible. I had arranged for him and my mom to move to Charlotte, where I now live, so they could be close to us, but anytime my mom and I put a plan together to help provide professional care for him, he would blow it up. He finally moved back to Moncks Corner, South Carolina, where I'd grown up, to live alone in his home. Even then, I lined up people to go and take care of him—but he fired them all. Four times.

We would get on the phone and try to talk to each other, and we would both end up yelling. Whenever I called him, he would go into a rage within two minutes. This went on for months. It was terrible. On Sundays I would get up and preach to my church, and on Tuesdays I'd have a shouting match with my dad. I felt like a hypocrite about it, but I couldn't figure out a way past it.

I knew what I wanted: reconciliation. I wanted to be by my dad's side. I wanted to be able to take care of him. The problem wasn't knowing what needed to happen. It rarely is. It was knowing how to get there. The issue was figuring out how to move forward in an impossibly complicated situation. I had tried everything I could think of, but we seemed to be stuck in anger and dysfunction.

Father's Day rolled around. I happened to be driving home from a vacation with my family. I remember being lost in thought as I drove, feeling bad that I couldn't be with my dad but also furious and hurt at how he had been treating all of us, especially my mom. Suddenly something my father-in-law had told me weeks earlier popped into my head. "Try to remember the good times. He did a lot of things right."

When he told me that, it was the last thing I wanted to hear. But that Father's Day, as I was driving down the same highway that went through Moncks Corner, I had an idea. I wasn't sure if it was a good one or not, but it was something I hadn't tried yet, and I wasn't ready to give up. I didn't want my dad to die without our relationship being restored, and I didn't know how much time I had left.

I asked Holly to drive, and I pulled out a piece of paper and a pen. I decided to write down one good memory for every year he had been my dad. I was thirty-two, so that meant listing thirty-two positive memories. I wasn't sure I could do it, to be honest. That's how mad I was. Even though he was a good dad and did far more than thirty-two positive things, I wasn't certain I could recall them at the moment. I was going to try, though, and I was going to drop off the list at his house when we drove through.

At first, I could hardly get a word on the page. My mind was full of all the abusive things he had said and done in the last few months, and it took a lot of effort to rewind the clock and think about my childhood. But as I moved the pen across the page in faith, as I did the thing that I would do if I had a good relationship with my dad, the memories and feelings I needed to access began to flow.

The first thing I remembered was when I played baseball as a kid. Dad was our coach, and we were so bad he wouldn't let any of us swing when we got up to bat. He made us bunt for the whole season. So I wrote down one word: "Bunting." That got me started.

Then I remembered a time when I was about fourteen years old and he took me to a punk rock concert in Ladson, South Carolina. He loved fishing, not punk rock, but he was trying to connect with me, and he knew I loved music. The concert was the worst music we had ever heard, but we were there together. I wrote down, "Punk rock concert, Ladson."

Now it was flowing. Next I remembered a time he took me to a revival meeting at a little country church. We had no idea what we were getting ourselves into. The guest speaker was an old-school fire-and-brimstone preacher, and we were seated in the front row. The preacher got really fired up, and people started hollering. At one point a little boy jumped up and shouted, but he didn't say, "Amen," "Praise the Lord," or "Preach it, preacher." He yelled, "Let the wild hog eat!" I had never heard that one before, and to be honest, I've never heard it since. I still don't know what he meant. I wrote it down. "Let the wild hog eat."

I finished the list just as we pulled into Moncks Corner. We drove up to the house, and I knocked on the door. I didn't even hug my dad when he opened it. I just handed him the paper. "Here. I made you a list. It's thirty-two things I remember about you."

I wish I could say we fell into each other's arms and reconciled on the spot, but this wasn't a Hallmark movie, and we were too stubborn and hurt by each other to do that. All I did was hand him the list, sit with him for ten minutes, and walk back to my car.

He called me later and asked, "How did you remember all this stuff?" We talked and laughed for a few minutes. It was a crack in the wall between us, a tiny way forward, and we both took it.

Not long after that, we truly made peace with each other. I was able to be with him when he passed away a few months later. I will forever be grateful that God didn't let me stop trying, that he kept nudging me forward even when I felt trapped.

As I think back over that Father's Day breakthrough, I can see the practicality and the power of this principle: "do the thing that you would do." By making that list, I did a mini version of the thing that I would have liked to do, which was to be able to talk with my dad. But since we couldn't talk without shouting, I wrote. I did the thing that I would have done if we both weren't so hurt, or at least something that pointed in that direction.

The second meaning of that phrase is even more important, though. I had to choose to act like "that me," the true me, the God-created me. The list the current version of me wanted to write would have been titled "32 Ways You've Let Us Down in the Last Two Years" or something like that. That felt natural, at least right then. But that's not the version of me I wanted to take into my dad's final days. It's not the version of me I knew God could see or that God was calling me into. So by his grace, I did the thing that *that* me would do. I humbled myself. I stirred up love. I took a risk. I tried one more time.

And God came through.

I'm not holding myself up as some sort of hero here—that idea came from God, after all. So did the grace to carry it out despite my hurt. So did my dad's response. So did our ultimate reconciliation. Yes, the two of us had to do our part, but we did it in partnership with a God who had always cared deeply about our relationship and whose power is greater than any brokenness or offense.

That's what gives me hope in every difficult circumstance, and it's what should give you hope too. You may not always be creative or strong or determined or holy or selfless or giving, but *God* is. He is what you need, and he has what you lack.

> You may not always be creative or strong or determined or holy or selfless or giving, but *God* is.

When you turn to him, you find the grace to step into a new, more mature, more patient, more expansive you.

I know God is going to keep nudging you forward as long as there is breath in your body. He's going to remove the layers of your old self and replace them with your true nature. He's going to challenge your defaults and expand your capacity for pressure. He's going to show you who you really are and lead you into the future he has always known, and you'll embrace it because it's more fully you.

The mindset "I'm not stuck unless I stop" is about commitment to progress. It's the decision the new you makes to not give up in the face of obstacles, but instead to lean on grace and look for the next step God has for you.

In other words, you can't do it without God, but God is not going to do it without you either. His power is flowing through you and his hand is leading you, so you will be enough for the task at hand. When you realize that Jesus makes you sufficient, you discover a new level of security, confidence, and self-acceptance.

It is this connection between Christ and us that lies at the heart of our second mindset, our second affirmation, which might be the most important one of all: *Christ is in me. I am enough.*

MINDSET (02)

CHRIST IS IN ME.
I AM ENOUGH.

ACTION STEP:
ACCEPT YOUR SELF.

SIX

MORE THAN WHAT YOU'RE MISSING

It was the 2016 Olympics, and the women's wrestling finals match was about to begin. Twenty-four-year-old American wrestler Helen Maroulis was standing in the tunnel leading into the arena. Next to her was her opponent, Japanese competitor Saori Yoshida, a three-time Olympic champ with thirteen world gold medals to her name and the clear favorite to take home the gold. Helen had faced Saori Yoshida twice before at other events and lost both times. But she had been training for three years for this moment.

"I've never felt anything like what it felt like before the finals match. It was electric," Helen recounted in an interview later, talking about how she stayed positive before stepping onto the mat. "I look over for one second, and I see Yoshida, and I turn back. I'm like, *Oh dang, Helen. Oh man.* Five seconds is enough for a bad thought to get into your mind or a negative thought or a doubt or anything. I'm like, *God, how do I protect myself right now?* So I had this mantra: Christ is in me. I am enough. Christ is in me. I am enough. Christ is in me. I am enough."*

Minutes later, Helen defeated Saori Yoshida 4-1 in one of the biggest upsets in wrestling history.

I love that story for two reasons. First, as the dad of a wrestler, I respect an Olympic gold medalist to the highest degree. Second, the mantra that Helen repeated is one that I preached about a few weeks before she won the Olympics. She was watching the message online, and to know that Helen wielded an affirmation from a sermon as she won Olympic gold made me smile.

Whether you're an Olympic wrestler, a single mother, a pastor, a mechanic, a schoolteacher, or a student, you often have to talk yourself *out* of some things and *into* others. You have to talk yourself out of doubt and into faith. Out of your weakness and into God's strength. Out of your head and into your future.

You don't face an opponent on a mat; you face obstacles in life. And instead of fighting once every four years, you find yourself wrestling every four *minutes* with another reason to doubt yourself. Another reason to wonder if you are enough. Another voice telling you to be stronger, smarter, funnier, prettier, thinner, richer, cooler, nicer. Another voice that focuses on how much you're missing and how often you fall short.

Sometimes, maybe a lot of the time, you might not feel like you're enough. Life is too big. It's too hard. It's beyond your control. You constantly try to juggle all the things you're

---

* FloWrestling, "Helen Maroulis Breaks Down Her Historic Win Over Saori Yoshida (Girls Can't Wrestle Ep. 2)" (YouTube, April 13, 2018), https://www .youtube.com/watch?v=-cvlGWA_eRY.

supposed to do, want to do, need to do—but sometimes it can feel like you drop more balls than you catch. You disappoint yourself, you let down those you care about, and you feel like the whole thing is set up to make you fail.

I think we've all heard an inner voice of failure, of worthlessness, and of lack. I know I have. Too many times I've found myself struggling to manage eighteen things at once, and none of them can be left undone because they are all interdependent. But I can't do it all. I don't have enough time. I don't have enough energy. I don't have enough patience. I don't have enough . . .

The list of "not enoughs" never ends.

Even worse, it's an easy jump from "I don't have enough" in a few areas of your life to "I am not enough" as a person. The first is just a statement about the situation you're going through. The other is a label that locks you into an old version of yourself.

In other words, you start to measure yourself in terms of what you're missing. You turn your insufficiency into your identity. You make your lack into your label.

Now, I'm sure you have good days too. I know there are areas where you are strong, seasons where things go right, victories that make you proud. As we saw earlier, those moments are often glimpses into the new you that God created you to be.

Those moments are encouraging, but they will never make you feel *enough*. Not for long, anyway. And they're not meant to.

Only God can do that.

That's why this mindset has two parts. "Christ is in me. I am enough." You can't have the second half without the first half.

Jesus told his disciples shortly before his death and resur-rection, "Because I live, you also will live. On that day you will realize that I am in my Father, and you are in me, and I am in you" (John 14:19–20). A few verses later, he said this famous phrase: "I am the vine; you are the branches. If you remain in me and I in you, you will bear much fruit; apart from me you can do nothing" (15:5).

Jesus was telling his disciples that their lives were in him, and he was in them—and that was what made them enough. Do you see the logic there? Can you hear the encouragement in Jesus' voice? He wasn't yelling at them, "Be holy enough! Be wise enough! Be pure enough! Be perfect enough!" He was saying, "*I* am enough. And because I'm with you, you will be enough."

He says the same thing to you. You are more than what you're missing or where you fall short. You have nothing to prove because your sufficiency comes from Christ, and he's never going to fail.

> You have nothing to prove because your sufficiency comes from Christ, and he's never going to fail.

Yes, you make mistakes and have weaknesses. We all do. Don't you think an all-knowing God knew that when he created you before the foundation of the world? Instead of blaming yourself, rejecting yourself, hating yourself, or running from yourself, you can accept yourself. Accept your true Self—with a capital S because it's the version of you that God cre-ated. It's the new you.

This mental switch into "I am not enough" happens eas-ily, usually without our realizing it. My son Elijah walked into the house one day and said he was planning a fishing trip with his friends. When I was a kid, my dad taught me to fish (or he tried to, anyway) but I didn't really enjoy it. I remember keeping score of how many times the fish would bite versus how many fish we caught as a way to dull the boredom. So, as a parent, I never really took my kids fishing.

When Elijah said he wanted to go with his friends, my brain jumped from "Cool, he wants to fish," to "He doesn't know how to fish," to "I never taught him to fish," to "I'm a bad dad because I never taught him to fish."

All this took place in a split second. Do you see what happened there? Suddenly the fact that Elijah didn't know enough about fishing meant I wasn't enough as a father.

Have you ever done that? You take an area where you don't measure up to some idealized expectation and you turn it into an identity. Then it all spirals from there. "If I were better at handling money, we wouldn't be twenty thousand dollars in debt. If I were a better parent, my son wouldn't be failing all his classes. If I were a better boss, we wouldn't have lost that contract to the competition. It's all my fault. I don't have enough because I'm not enough."

I'm not saying to delude yourself into thinking you're perfect. I'm not saying you and I couldn't have made some better choices along the way. But let's show ourselves some compassion. Let's give ourselves some credit. Maybe you are doing a really good job, but you've been hit by some unexpected blows. Don't internalize those losses and convince yourself that *you* are not enough.

There's a Taylor Swift lyric that says, "I'm the problem, it's me." Some of us have that phrase on repeat in our heads. (And in case you were wondering, I know that lyric thanks to my twelve-year-old daughter.) The background track to our day is, "I'm the problem. It's me. My home isn't clean enough. My job doesn't pay enough. I don't negotiate well enough with clients. I didn't try hard enough to make my marriage work. I don't have enough time, enough energy, enough self-discipline, enough credit, enough experience. Yeah, I'm the problem here. It's me."

Now, if you really are part of the problem, recognize it and work on it. You're not stuck unless you stop, remember? But my point is that you can't jump to dramatic, generalized, self-deprecatory conclusions about yourself every time you go through challenges or make mistakes. Instead of assuming you are broken and bad beyond repair, learn to accept your God-designed, God-created Self as God accepts you and then work toward a better result in whatever areas need to improve.

When Elijah made that comment about fishing, I got over my insecurity pretty quickly. I think I said something like, "Sorry I didn't teach you how to be a fisherman, Elijah. But hey, I showed you how to be a *fisher of men*!" It was a dad joke and a preacher joke rolled into one. Now you know what my family has to live with.

The point I'm trying to make is that you have to find your sufficiency in Jesus and stop the downward spiral of despair. His abundant life is already within you. Out of his abundance, he is providing the resources you need. Enough is not a state you will eventually reach. It is a gift you have already been given.

> Enough is not a state you will eventually reach. It is a gift you have already been given.

If you've bought into the belief that what makes you enough is *what you do* or *what you have*, you're always going to be operating from a deficit because, honestly, life is too much for any of us. That's what God wanted Moses to understand when he introduced himself as, "I am who I am" (Exodus 3:14). He was trying to get Moses to see that God's very nature is "enoughness." It's sufficiency. It's abundance.

He's trying to get us to trust him in the same way. The first step to accepting your Self is realizing just how "enough" God really is. It's his presence, not our performance, that makes us approved.

"I'm not enough" is a wrong way of thinking. It's an old mindset, part of the former self that you are called to put off. You might not feel like you're enough right now, but in Christ you are more than a conqueror, so *you are enough*. You might not think you have enough to meet the need at hand, but God supplies all your needs in Christ Jesus, so *you will have enough*.

That's why Paul wrote, "I have been crucified with Christ and I no longer live, but Christ lives in me. The life I now live in the body, I live by faith in the Son of God, who loved me and gave himself for me" (Galatians 2:20). He knew that Christ in him was the deciding factor. Salvation was his defining moment. No matter what might come his way in the future, his sense of worth and security were connected to Christ. He knew he'd be enough.

And you will too. That's the promise of the Bible.

Do you really think God would just drop you into your life and not put within you the things you need for what he has called you to do? When you don't feel like you're enough, don't fall into the trap of trying to be everything and do everything on your own. Tell yourself, "I am enough because

God knew I would be here. He knew what I would need for this situation. If he put me in the situation, he put his strength in me."

As Helen Maroulis said, all it takes is five seconds for negativity and doubt to get into your head. Your sense of sufficiency and worth is under constant attack by a world that doesn't know the new you. So focus less on your lack and more on God's abundance.

God is enough, and he gives you enough and makes you enough. He fed Israel manna from heaven for forty years. He gave them water from a rock in the desert. He told ravens to feed Elijah during a famine. Jesus turned water into wine at a wedding. He had a fish pay for Peter's taxes. He fed thousands of people from a little boy's lunch. He told the disciples exactly where to cast their nets and they pulled in the biggest catch they'd ever experienced.

I could go on and on. God isn't running out of resources. If he showed up for the men and women in the Bible, he'll show up for you. If they asked for it, you can ask for it. If they believed for it, you can believe for it. God gives you what you need, when you need it, so that you can do what he asks you to do.

I'll say it again. *You* are enough.

Not some idealized, impossibly perfect version of you. Not the person you wish you were. Not the person your parents told you that you should be. Not the person you're pretending to be. Not the person in your Tinder profile or Instagram posts.

You. Today. Right now.

You are already accepted by God. You already have the mind of Christ. The Spirit already dwells in you. God's promises are already yours. Don't say you're *not* enough: say you're *now* enough. That's how God sees you, and that's what Christ makes you.

You're not done changing, of course. You are being conformed and transformed into his image every day, so there are some habits and immaturities you still have to leave behind. But in your essence, at your core, you are who you need to be because you are handmade by God. You are the handiwork of the divine. He made you on purpose. That is the you that you need to accept because it is the one God made.

> You are the handiwork of the divine. He made you on purpose. That is the you that you need to accept because it is the one God made.

Remember, you are much more than whatever it is you think you're missing. Your lack cannot label you. Your deficiency doesn't define you. Your need doesn't get to name you. You are defined by the One who created you and resides inside you, the great "I Am That I Am," the God who supplies all your needs according to his riches in glory.

The God who knows you is the One who chose you, so you have nothing to prove, no one to impress, nobody to fear. He calls you by name. He knows the hairs on your head and the thoughts of your heart. He values you, loves you, fills you, empowers you. He sees the power and potential he put within you.

Do you?

SEVEN

TRICKS ARE FOR KIDS

When I was nine, my mom took me to the trading card shop in Moncks Corner. She waited in the car while I went inside and bought a pack of basketball cards. I was so excited I opened it right there at the counter. Immediately I recognized the name on one card—Michael Jordan.

The owner of the store was watching me, and when he saw it, he leaned over the counter and said, "Hey, I'll trade you a second pack of cards for just that one card."

That seemed like a no-brainer to my nine-year-old self. "A whole pack for one card? Sure!" I handed him the card, he gave me another pack, and I walked out of the store thinking I had gotten the best deal ever.

When I got back to the car, my mom asked how it went. When I told her I got two packs, she was immediately suspicious. "How did you get two? I only gave you money for one."

"You'll never believe it, Mom! He gave me a whole new pack for one card."

"Steven," she said, "what card was it?"

"Michael Jordan," I told her.

Her face changed immediately. She told me to wait in the car, then she marched into the store. Five minutes later, she came back with my Michael Jordan card—and a third pack of cards.

You see, my mom knew the value of that card. So did the owner. But I didn't, so I fell for a trick. I traded away something valuable because I was too inexperienced and immature to recognize the worth of what I had in my hand.

I wonder, how often do we trade away our God-given identity because we don't know our own worth? We fall for the lie that we don't matter that much. The devil tells us we're irredeemably flawed, and we believe him. Society and culture tell us that our worth is in our appearance, and we believe them. Our own minds whisper that we are frauds and imposters, and we believe ourselves.

And we fall for tricks.

We give away what really matters and chase after what doesn't. Instead of cards, we hand over our character. We hand over our calling. We hand over our confidence. We lose our peace in the pursuit of pleasure. We exchange our joy for stress, our generosity for fear, our good reputation for five minutes of popularity.

Do you remember the iconic cereal slogan, "Silly rabbit! Trix are for kids"? I grew up in the eighties, and this was one of the catchiest marketing campaigns of my childhood. Not only was it catchy, it was true. *Tricks* are for kids. Immaturity and lack of experience are the things that con artists and tricksters prey upon.

That's why I let go of a Michael Jordan card, and it's why we often let go of our Self: the person God says we are. If we don't know who we are and value what God has put in us, we'll get tricked into trading that all away for things that don't matter.

There's a powerful Bible story about Jacob convincing Esau to give up his birthright. Jacob and Esau were brothers. As the firstborn, Esau was entitled to authority, inheritance, and leadership in the family. But one day, after being out on a hunting trip, he came home hungry and found Jacob cooking stew. Esau's stomach took over. He ended up trading his birthright to Jacob for a bowl of stew, which has to be the worst trade in history. The Bible says he "despised his birthright" by doing that (Genesis 25:34).

> If we don't know who we are and value what God has put in us, we'll get tricked into trading that all away for things that don't matter.

It's easy to criticize Esau, but we do the same thing when we sell ourselves short by not valuing who God made us to be. We don't do this on purpose any more than Esau planned to trade away his birthright. Esau's desire to eat and his fear of dying got the best of him. He was immature and unwise. So he fell for a trick.

That's why you have to continually grow in your knowledge of you. And it's why learning to "do the new you" doesn't happen overnight. Do you want to avoid tricks? Learn how valuable you really are so you don't settle for less than you were called to be. Get around people who will remind you of your true worth and reflect it back to you. Spend time mining your sense of significance from the Word of God.

Listen to the Creator himself and get his acceptance of you deep into your soul.

Say it out loud if you can. *Christ is in me. I am enough.* Put on this mindset. Take responsibility to change the way you see yourself and talk about yourself. After all, your voice is the one you hear the most often and the one that affects you the most deeply.

Often, the tricks that trip us up are of our own making. We don't need the devil to lie to us: we're doing a fine job of it all on our own. "I can't do that. I'm never going to be able to do this. I shouldn't even try. I'll mess things up. Someone else would do a better job anyway."

To be honest, we often have good reason to be pessimistic: we live with ourselves. We have a front-row seat to our mistakes and missteps. If we focus only on that, and if we forget that Christ in us is what makes us sufficient, our frailty and fallibility can make a very convincing argument that we'll never be enough for what God has called us to step into.

I remember when I accepted Jesus at the age of sixteen. It was an easy decision, at least for the most part. At first, I wrestled with it because I wondered if following Christ would cost too much, but when it came down to it, what's not to accept? Salvation is the best deal ever. Jesus paid for my sins. He took away my shame. He gave me his resurrection power. He prays for me when I don't have the words to say. Who wouldn't want that?

What's been a lot harder for me than accepting Jesus is accepting *Steven*. Accepting Jesus took a moment; accepting me is taking a lifetime.

Steven is far from perfect. He's not always forgiving. He doesn't have all wisdom. He lets people down. He's five-foot-eight-and-a-half wearing boots with heels, which seems to disappoint people. "Huh, you looked taller on-screen," they always say.

Every day I live with Steven, I discover a few more things I don't like. More things I wish I could change. More things God needs to fix.

Now, there's good stuff in me too. This isn't false humility or a pity tactic. I believe I help a lot of people. Holly says I'm an awesome husband, and I think my kids are pretty happy to have me as a dad. But as I said before, I'm so far from the person I want to be (IDIOT!). And the more I learn, the more I realize how little I know. The more I grow, the more I see how far I have to go.

I try really hard to be like Jesus, but at the end of the day, I'm still Steven.

What I've realized, though, is that to accept Jesus but not to accept Steven is to miss the gift of salvation where it matters the most. You can't just accept Jesus by faith. You have to accept your Self by faith. Sure, you're a work in progress. But you are beautiful, valuable, and important right now too.

David wrote, "I praise you because I am fearfully and wonderfully made; your works are wonderful, I know that full well . . . How precious to me are your thoughts, God! How vast is the sum of them!" (Psalm 139:14, 17). David made some massive mistakes, but he knew how valuable his life was to God. He never forgot how much he was worth.

Do you know your worth? Do you value your Self? Have you accepted that you are valuable beyond description to

God? Are you committed to loving your Self, showing grace to your Self, stepping into your Self, and trusting God with your Self? Or do you see yourself as less than others, as not enough, as disposable, replaceable, forgettable? That's the message the enemy will try to give you, but it's not what God says about you.

At the card shop, the guy at the counter knew the value of his cards because he had a book that told him how much they were worth. If I could have looked up my Michael Jordan card in that book, I wouldn't have traded it away for a one-dollar pack of worthless cards.

You have a book that tells you *your* value. Have you read it? Have you looked yourself up in that book? Did you read the part where Jesus gave his life for you because you're worth so much to him? Did you see where it says that the Holy Spirit lives in you? Did you read that you have a calling and a future, that God has given you gifts and grace that are unique to you, and you have to use those gifts because nobody else can do what you do?

If you look yourself up in the book, you'll see that you are precious in the sight of God. You are more than a conqueror. You have the mind of Christ. You are called according to his purpose.

Don't settle for less than that!

If you have made any trades that you regret, if you've let your character slip or your confidence weaken or your calling fade, it's time to reclaim the version of you that is rightfully yours. The Holy Spirit will walk into the card shop and tell the devil to give you your peace back, your joy back, your dream back, your kindness back, your courage back, your passion back, your creativity back, your song back. You might have thought they were gone, but they are part of the true you, the new you, and nobody can take them if you refuse to trade them.

Learn who you are in Christ and step into that version of your Self. It's who you were meant to be, and it's perfect. Don't let anybody tell you anything different.

EIGHT

I AM WHAT I AM

I remember taking New Testament Greek in college. Actually, what I mostly remember is *dropping* New Testament Greek a few weeks after I started taking it. I was a mass communication major, not a religion major, so Greek wasn't a requirement, but I had signed up anyway hoping to get ahead for my future seminary plans. Then I realized how hard it was, and I decided to drop out.

So, one afternoon after classes were over, I walked into the professor's classroom with a slip from my adviser who was helping me drop the class and take something easier. The professor was standing there with another religion teacher, and their response was, "Well, Furtick, we knew it wouldn't take long, but you dropped this class even quicker than we expected!"

They were kind of joking around, but there was an undertone of "We knew you weren't a serious enough student to do this kind of disciplined work."

Now I'm sure I was reading into it a little bit because I felt bad about dropping the class. But to this day, I have a nagging voice in my head that tells me I'm not "deep" enough. A lot of times when I'm preparing to preach, it's as if those two professors were standing there, taunting me in my mind, telling me to prove that I'm deep enough and disciplined enough.

I'm not saying they meant that. I'm not saying I can't take a joke. I'm not even saying I shouldn't have pushed through and finished the class. But my point is that sometimes things get into us more than we realize, more than we can name or know as they're happening.

The things that damage your self-acceptance don't come into your life fully grown. They start as tiny seeds, as subtle ideas or comments that you don't even question at first. A teacher told you in second grade that you weren't good at math. An ex-boyfriend made you feel like the breakup was your fault, and you believe you're bad at relationships. Someone in high school made fun of your voice and now you're self-conscious anytime you sing.

My daughter, Abbey, told me the other day that she hates her ears. When I asked her why, I found out her brothers had said her ears were too big. Naturally, that led to a very direct conversation with the boys. I definitely don't want my daughter going around ashamed of her ears, of all things. I don't want a little seed planted in her that turns into a serious self-image problem later in life.

You see, over time, seeds of self-rejection grow. You water them every time you agree with them, until eventually they turn into invasive weeds that choke out who you really are. You start to despise parts of you because you fall short of what you "should" be.

But who gets to define what you "should" be? Shouldn't it be the one who created you? The one who chose you before time began, who loves you more than you love yourself, who knows you better than you know yourself? The mindset we're looking at, "Christ is in me. I am enough," is about learning not just to tolerate the person God made you to be, but to celebrate it and to fully and unapologetically step into it.

The problem with not accepting your Self is that you carry that deficit into every situation. You're always on the defensive. Always trying to prove something. Always holding insecurity at bay. Always standing over the invisible abyss of an imagined worthlessness.

That's the opposite of abundant life!

But all too often, it becomes normal. It becomes your default. Somewhere along the way, a "not enough" tag can get slapped on an area of your life, and you end up carrying that label for years without stopping to ask if it's true.

This matters because it affects how you handle challenges and opportunities. For example, if I'm constantly fighting a voice that tells me I'm not deep enough as a preacher, or that I'm not serious enough or I'm not a hard worker, then all that defensiveness is going to come out in how I preach and teach. I'll subconsciously think, "Oh, this needs to be deep. *I* need to be deep. I can't get on that platform and be shallow. I've got to prove the people wrong who said I'm not deep."

That's not going to help at all, though. If anything, it will block me from hearing from God. It will keep me from seeing those I'm really ministering to and lock me into a cycle of trying to prove something to professors from the past who aren't even in my life anymore. I will get in my own head. I will make it all about proving something instead of serving someone.

Now, I feel a little vulnerable telling you all this. I know it's specific to my calling and role. But I bet you've experienced the same dynamic. You can tell you're operating from a place of "not enough" by asking yourself: Where am I trying to prove myself instead of just *being* myself? Where am I forgetting that God's power is in my presence, not my perfection? In fully showing up as I am and trusting that he is enough in me? Where do I need to get out of my head and into God's grace?

What I should be saying to myself before I preach is, "God has taught me a lot. God has given me a gift and I've done what is in my power to learn and grow in that gift. He knows the people I need to help, and he will put me in front of those people today because they matter to him. This isn't even about me. It's about them, and it's about Christ working through me."

It works the same way in your marriage, in your character, in your business startup, in your walk with God. What you need is inside you because Christ is inside you. God put it there. He prepared you for this moment. You've trained for this. Maybe you failed in the past, but you're not who you used to be. You've grown into this. Silence the inner critic, the distracting chatter, the voices that say, "I knew you'd quit. I knew you'd fail. It was only a matter of time."

Are you facing something intimidating? Are the negative consequences of failure filling your mind? Silence the chatter. Focus your faith. You can do this. God prepared you and trained you for this, and he's with you all the way.

I know we all feel like imposters once in a while. The inner questioning is not always a bad thing—it keeps us honest and humble and hungry. But if we are more focused on proving we are not frauds than on being our real selves, something needs to change.

I think the apostle Paul felt like an imposter sometimes, but he knew how to process it. He knew how to trade his insufficiency for Christ's sufficiency. He wrote, "For I am the least of the apostles and do not even deserve to be called an apostle, because I persecuted the church of God. But by the grace of God I am what I am, and his grace to me was not without effect. No, I worked harder than all of them—yet not I, but the grace of God that was with me" (1 Corinthians 15:9–10).

Paul recognized his own efforts and success. He didn't say, "I can't do anything right. I'm a total failure. I'm a terrible apostle." No, he was proud of what he had done. But he didn't base his identity on his activity.

Instead, he turned to grace. He leaned on grace. He rested in grace.

In essence he was saying, "I am what I am by the grace of God, and that grace is powerful. That grace is effective. That grace is unique to me, so I'm going to walk in it confi-

> Instead of listening to your lack, agree with God's abundance.

dently, but at the end of the day, I don't have anything to prove. I can set aside what I accomplished and rest in what God accomplished."

Instead of listening to your lack, agree with God's abundance. Say to yourself, "I am what I am by the grace of God. His grace is enough. I have all I need because he is all I need."

Of course, if you're going to believe that you are enough, you have to learn how to silence the voice of comparison. Comparison is a killer. It's a liar. It's a thief. It steals your confidence and joy in who you are by telling you that because you *have* less than someone else or *do* less than someone else, you *are* less.

My weight-lifting buddy Buck sent Elijah and me a workout the other day. It was ridiculous. If we would have tried to do what Buck wanted us to do, it would have ended in injury or vomit or both. So I told Elijah what Buck wanted us to do, and then I told him what we were actually going to do, and it was about half of what Buck had sent over.

Elijah looked at me funny, like maybe we were compromising by cutting the workout in half. I said, "Elijah, don't feel bad. Buck is just built different."

Years ago, I might have felt bad about modifying the routine. Not anymore. I know who I am, and I know who I'm not, and I'm not Buck. There is only one Buck. Some would call him a psychopath, some would call him an elite athlete. There's a fine line. He's just built different.

So are you.

God planned you. God produced you. And God is proud of you.

Where do you feel like you are not enough? In your money managing skills? In your parenting? In your exercise habits? In your career? In what areas or scenarios do you hear a nagging, accusing voice that tells you something is wrong with you, you need to get your act together, you are the problem?

Maybe there isn't a problem. *Maybe you're just built different.* You're not less than, more than, better than, or worse than anyone else. You're you. The you that God knew you needed to be. Don't compare your parenting style to the other classroom mom who made gluten-free zebra-shaped cookies on field trip day. You are the mom your kids need and love. Don't compare your creativity to the other creative people you've met. Be creative in your own way. Besides, you never know the secret cost of someone else's creativity or the grind that goes into their greatness. Comparison will steal your contentment. Don't fall for it.

Now, if you need to change in some area, God will make that clear, and he'll give you the power and grace to step into that new version of you. As I said earlier, you are loved as you are, but you don't have to remain there. You are fully accepted by God today, but you can still become a more authentic version of you with each passing day.

Accepting your Self is not about never changing, but rather about believing you are perfectly loved and accepted right now, and there is nothing you could do to make God love you more. It's about believing that God knows your weaknesses and the challenges you face, and he will show himself strong through them. It's about refusing to let the devil tell you that you are not enough. That's not how God talks or what God says, so it's not the way he's going to motivate you to change.

> Accepting your Self is not about never changing, but rather about believing you are perfectly loved and accepted right now, and there is nothing you could do to make God love you more.

I still can't read Greek like my old professor, and I probably never will. I can't lift weights like Buck, and I don't even want to. I can't wrestle like Helen, but I can sure cheer her on. There are so many things I can't do—but that's okay. I've made peace with it. I am who I am by the perfect, potent, and permanent grace of God.

And so are you.

So accept your Self. Embrace who you are. Love who God made you. Work on it, too, of course. Practice being the best version of you, the version that matches God's vision. Grow into the person who God already knows you, and enables you, to be.

Christ is the grace of God in you. And his presence makes you enough.

NINE

COMING FROM ABUNDANCE

One night when he was really young, Elijah grabbed five napkins at dinner. Five. He wasn't handing them out to the family either. I'm talking about one kid. One meal. Five napkins.

I hate to say it, but I started to freak out a little. Frugality is one thing, but I was fussing about it with a little more intensity than the situation warranted. I stopped myself, though. Why was this such a huge issue to me in that moment? Shouldn't I be glad he was keeping his face and hands clean instead of using his shirt and pants like he used to? Why was I triggered by napkins, of all things?

Then I remembered how my dad would always tear paper towels in half at dinner. He'd tell us, "You don't need a whole paper towel sheet. Half of one is enough. Learn how to get by with half." He grew up very poor, so he was serious about frugality. He drilled it into us. And some of his aversion to waste was really healthy. Some of it was over the top, though.

As I watched Elijah go through napkins like he didn't even care that they could run out, I realized something. Without thinking about it, I had carried my dad's napkin scarcity mentality into my own adulthood, where it no longer applied.

And that, right there, was the problem: *I hadn't thought about it.*

Until I did.

And then I realized I was being petty and needed to loosen up a little bit. I still think five napkins is overkill, though.

I wonder, though—are there any areas where you are carrying around a scarcity mindset, and you haven't stopped to think about it? Where you've never questioned why you are so afraid, so defensive, so petty?

I'm not talking about the number of napkins you need at dinner. I'm talking about the way you see your resources. The way you see your marriage. The way you manage your finances. The way you plan your schedule. The way you discipline your kids. The way you treat your employees. The way you dream for the future. The way you use your free time.

Do you approach life from a place of lack? Or a place of abundance?

See, the connection between "Christ is in me" and "I am enough" is meant to be one of abundance. I can't imagine Jesus keeping track of napkins at the Last Supper. He turned a picnic lunch into a meal for a multitude. He wasn't really worried about running out of stuff.

So why am I? Why are you? Why do we so often look at life through the filter of not enough?

> Do you approach life from a place of lack? Or a place of abundance?

In Brené Brown's book *The Gifts of Imperfection*, she talks about how "never enough" is the mantra that describes how so many of us feel in almost every area of our life. I couldn't agree more. When I feel anxious or irritable or insecure or hopeless, I can usually connect it to a starting place of *never enough.* "I never get enough sleep. I never have enough money. I never have enough time. I never have enough energy." If I take that kind of thought process into my interactions with my family or into my work, it's a disaster waiting to happen.

Jesus said he came to give life and life more abundantly. That means the new you can go into the day from a place of abundance, not lack. You have to *put on* that mindset, though. You have to decide to tap into the you that comes from abundance. If you keep talking about how you never get enough sleep, you'll always feel tired. If you keep complaining about not having enough time, you'll always feel stressed out. Your inner dialogue matters, so reframe the challenges you face in light of God's abundance.

I'm not saying you should deny reality. If you only slept three hours last night, you probably can't talk yourself into feeling rested. What I'm saying is, don't make "never enough" the mindset you filter your day through. Don't make "I'm not enough" the foundation you make your decisions by. Otherwise, you'll go to bed at night stressed, and you'll wake up tired because your stress kept you from resting, and you'll repeat the never-enough cycle day after day.

What does coming from abundance look like? It looks like believing when you wake up every morning that you will have enough time and energy for what God has called you to do today. God gives you the grace you need for each day, and remembering that truth will keep you from going into the day already defeated.

I'm sure you know that feeling: "I'm so busy. I'm so stressed. There's no way I'm going to get it all done today." I've got news for you. You *won't* get it all done today. Or tomorrow. Thank God for that because it gives him a reason to leave you on the earth another twenty-four hours! But seriously, life is too unpredictable and our plates are too full to expect to get it all done right away.

Take some of the pressure off and focus on what God wants you to do now. Sit with God's priorities. Sit with your to-do list. Sit with the people who are important in your life and figure out how best to live. Talk yourself through it. "Yesterday I got offtrack with this. It wasn't fruitful. So today, I'm going to prune out some stuff so I can bear the right fruit. These are the things that matter. This is what's important. This is what I can't do anything about, and this is what I can."

On a practical level, how do you come into your day from abundance? First, get clear in your heart the *priorities* God has for you.

Jesus said, "Seek first his kingdom and his righteousness, and all these things will be given to you as well" (Matthew 6:33). So if you feel like you aren't enough, start by evaluating whether you have the right desires and expectations. Does God really want you to have that house you're working so hard to afford? Do you have to spend that many hours at work? Do you have to answer emails at eight o'clock at night when your kids want to play Mario Kart with you?

Now, the things that deplete you, that pull from you, that seem to suck the energy and passion out of your very being— they aren't all bad. They force you to evaluate where you're going to put the resources God has given you. Don't shy away from things just because they're hard, but at the same time, don't pour all your energy and time into things that don't matter that much in the long run. God will give you enough resources for what you're meant to do, so if you don't have enough time or energy, it might not be a resource problem. It might be a priority problem.

Second, you come from abundance when you stay in God's *presence*. Inviting Jesus into your heart and life means a lot more than just salvation from sins. It means you have his power and presence inside of you wherever you go and whatever you face.

Jesus said, "Here I am! I stand at the door and knock" (Revelation 3:20). We use that verse to teach kids that they can ask Jesus into their hearts and be saved. That's true. But Jesus was talking to *believers* in this passage, not to people who needed to accept him for the first time. He was telling us that even if we've known him for many years, there is deeper intimacy and power available.

What challenge are you facing today? You have great needs, but you have a greater God who lives in you and flows through you. Paul said, "I can do all things through Christ who strengthens me" (Philippians 4:13 NKJV). Notice he didn't say, "*Christ* can do all things." That would be true, but he said Christ strengthens *you* so you can face all the things that need your attention. That parenting challenge. That lawsuit you were just served. That doctor's report you're waiting for. Whatever the day holds, Christ is always with you.

> You have great needs, but you have a greater God who lives in you and flows through you.

Here's a third way to come from abundance: *proactivity.*
Don't just sit back and wait for life to happen. Make progress
on what God is showing you. Maybe that means making a
budget. Maybe it means making a phone call. Maybe it means
asking a certain person out on a date. Do the thing that you
would do if you knew you would be up for the challenge.

Fear will try to paralyze you, but faith in God's abundance will empower you. If you believe God is with you, if
you believe he's faithful to his word, if you believe he's given
you all you need, then take action. The Bible says that "faith
by itself, if it is not accompanied by action, is dead" (James
2:17). Do what the faith-filled version of you would do
because that's the real you.

Finally, coming from abundance means having *patience.*
Sometimes you have to work for a long time before you see
the result. If you're coming from a
place of lack, that kind of delay
becomes desperation and then
despair. But a mindset of abundance
means you trust that God will do
the right work, at the right time, the
right way. There's no need to panic.

> Seeds have their own
> schedule, and so do
> God's promises.

There's another passage in James that says, "Be patient,
then, brothers and sisters, until the Lord's coming. See how
the farmer waits for the land to yield its valuable crop,
patiently waiting for the autumn and spring rains. You too,
be patient and stand firm, because the Lord's coming is near"
(5:7–8).

I don't know a lot about agriculture, but I do know that
not everything you plant will come up at the same time or in

the same way. Seeds have their own schedule, and so do God's promises.

A lot of things are beyond your control. Instead of forcing things, often you have to farm them. You have to water them. You have to wait for them.

If you tried to talk to your teenage daughter who is mad at you and she blew you off, be patient. Don't rise to her level of emotion. Keep loving her and reaching out to her. You'll get through this. Don't force it. Farm it.

If the book you are writing, the business you are building, the illness you are facing, or the trauma you are healing from is taking longer than you expected, be patient. Don't force it. Farm it.

Christ is in you, so you are enough. You can come from abundance if you seek God's *priorities*, rely on his *presence*, stay *proactive* by taking steps of faith, and remain *patient* in the process.

What challenge are you facing? In what areas has "never enough" felt like a mantra on repeat in your mind? You don't have to live from lack. Stop counting your kids' napkins and start counting the blessings they are in your life.

Then step into the abundant version of you. The you that comes from abundance *is* the real you.

I'm pretty sure I will never win an Olympic gold medal like Helen Maroulis, but I have my own challenges, and so do you. Maybe you wrestle with anxiety. Or you wrestle with credit card debt. Or you wrestle with temptation. Or you wrestle with your calling. Or you wrestle your toddler into bed after a long day.

Whatever challenge you're struggling with right now, whatever negativity might be trying to get into your head, make this the mindset you rest in, believe from, and fight with: *Christ is in me. I am enough.*

This confidence in God's presence and your purpose will lead you into action. It will carry you to victory because when you truly believe God is with you, you start to see obstacles as possibilities. You find yourself dreaming about the future, not just trying to survive the present.

A focus on possibility is the essence of the next mindset I want to share with you: *With God there is always a way, and by faith I will find it.*

WITH GOD THERE'S ALWAYS A WAY, AND BY FAITH I WILL FIND IT.

ACTION STEP:
FOCUS ON POSSIBILITY.

TEN

FORWARD, NOT FINISHED

A friend of mine named Rick Beato has one of my favorite YouTube channels. Rick tells the best stories about musicians, and he breaks down music theory in a fascinating way. When you listen to him talk about what makes a song great, it's so infectious that even if you didn't like the song before Rick explained it, it'll be one of your favorite songs by the time he finishes.

When I first started watching his channel with my son Graham, Rick had less than fifty thousand subscribers. Today he has over three million. A YouTuber with millions of subscribers is not that uncommon. But what makes Rick's story special is that he was fifty-four years old when he started the channel.

Recently I asked Rick, "Are you shocked by your success?" After all, he joined the social media world in his mid-fifties with a head of gray hair and more than half his life behind him. That doesn't happen every day.

He laughed and began to tell me his story. I knew some of it already, but as he shared the details, I was even more inspired.

Rick had been a music producer for a couple of decades, and he had experienced varying levels of success. But there came a point when things weren't going very well in the music business in general. Major label recording budgets were drying up. The work he was doing had started to feel dull and less interesting to him. He shared with me that he felt a little depressed and unsure of what to do in the future.

In the meantime, Rick happened to post a video on Facebook of his son Dylan, who was eight at the time, demonstrating perfect pitch. Now, if you don't know, perfect pitch is the ability to hear a music note and name it by ear, without having to play it on an instrument. It's a pretty cool thing to see, especially when it's an eight-year-old calling out the most complex chords effortlessly and rapidly. If you haven't seen it, search it. I promise you'll be blown away.

The video of Dylan went viral. Then, one day, Rick's intern happened to suggest, "You know, Rick, you really should start a YouTube channel."

Rick said he thought it was a crazy idea. "I looked around, and there was nobody with gray hair like mine on YouTube. I was a producer. I was a music teacher. That's what I did. I was a behind-the-scenes guy. In all my years of producing, I never allowed people to take pictures or video of me. That's the way I wanted it. So the idea of making videos seemed ridiculous. I didn't even know how to make videos."

By the time you're fifty-four, you usually have a pretty clear idea of what you can and can't do. You have a summary in your head of what you're good at and what you're terrible at, what you like and what you don't like. Actually, you don't have to be fifty-four to come to these conclusions. Most of us are writing mental summaries of ourselves from the time we're in middle school. "I'm shy. I'm not good at reading. I suck at sports. I can't make friends."

The beautiful thing about Rick is that he was willing to reinvent himself. He decided to start creating videos about anything and everything music related. At first, few people watched them. But eventually, several months in, some of them started to gain traction. Slowly but surely, Rick's channel became one of the premier spots on the internet—or anywhere—for music lovers and learners to gather. Rick has now interviewed some of the most famous guitarists of all time, including Dominic Miller, the guitarist for Sting, Brian May of Queen, Billy Corgan of the Smashing Pumpkins, Peter Frampton, and dozens more. I've heard renowned guitarists admit that they get nervous when Rick Beato reviews one of their songs on YouTube.

So many other YouTubers are younger and grew up in a digital, social media–infused world. How does Rick compete with (and even beat) the best of them? I think it's because— along with his insane work ethic and tremendous talent—he was willing to believe there was more to his story. He was willing to suck at something at first in order to find out what it could be. He was willing to put himself out there in a new way, to see himself differently than he had ever seen himself before, in order to have a greater impact and become a professor of music to millions in the second act of his life.

Now let me ask you a question. Are you willing to wander out into that kind of *what if*? What stories have you told yourself about your current situation or abilities? What summary have you written in your head about what you are good at and bad at, what you like and don't like, what you can and can't do? What have you assumed to be true and final about your circumstances? I'm not just talking about a career change either, but about any situation where you can't see a way *forward* so you've started wondering if you're *finished*.

It's one thing to be self-aware and humble. But it's another to resign yourself to your current state as if your story were over. As if the book of your life were already closed and nothing more could be added. I promise you, as long as your heart is beating and air is filling your lungs, you're not finished if you're willing to move forward.

The foundational step to this mindset is openness. "With God there's always a way, and by faith I will find it!" To walk in that truth, you have to stay open. If God wants to reinvent you, will you let him do it? If he wants to heal you, will you let him in? If he wants to redeem what you've given up on, will you let him have his way?

We may *say* yes to all these questions, but the real test comes when God sends us an opportunity. In Rick's case, it was an intern saying, "You should have a YouTube channel." There was no guarantee that it would reach massive levels of success. Rick had no way of knowing what was ahead of him. Neither do you. And you don't have to. But you do have to be open. You have to allow yourself the mental space to consider, *What if I could do this? What if this is God? What if this opportunity is not a pipe dream? What if this step I'm taking today actually matters? What if it's leading somewhere that God has known all along?*

To you it feels like reinvention, but to God it's a continuation. It's who you've always been. It's still your story; it's just the next chapter of you.

Remember the first mindset we looked at? You're only stuck if you stop. So what makes you stop? Often, it's a loss of hope. It's the discouragement and disappointment that come when you feel like there's no way forward.

Sometimes it's not one big disappointment or crushing discouragement. It's paralysis by papercut. Maybe you've been shut down so many times that you shut down your potential for progress in order to avoid the possibility of disappointment.

This mindset points you back to the God of hope and forward into the future he has in store. In him, there is always a way, and by faith you'll find it. When you are tempted to lose hope, don't go back to your old self. Don't settle for old definitions, old limitations, old labels.

Put on your new self. Do the thing that you would do if you believed there was a way, because God is about to open one.

> You make plans, but God makes paths.

Remember, though, this commitment to possibility is not something you do on your own. Proverbs says, "In their hearts humans plan their course, but the LORD establishes their steps." (16:9). Yes, you should make plans. That's one of the first signs you actually have faith. And it's wise. But just because you make your plans doesn't mean you make your way.

God does that.

You make plans, but God makes paths.

Sometimes we get so distracted and discouraged looking for the way forward that we forget about the Waymaker. As we are moving through challenges, we can't forget to look up and see the salvation of the Lord. Psalms says, "I lift up my eyes to the mountains—where does my help come from? My help comes from the LORD, the Maker of heaven and earth" (121:1).

Our God is a God of possibilities and paths, of redefinitions and reinventions, of wonderful works and unforeseen ways. If he needs a road, he'll make one. If he wants to move a mountain, he'll cast it into the sea. He built the world and he runs the world.

Maybe you got fired, but God didn't. He has the same job he had before you ever showed up on Earth. Maybe you don't have the family background you wish you had. God put you exactly where you needed to be. Quit telling yourself you're finished before you've even started. Quit voting yourself off the island before you've even played the game.

God runs things. He doesn't check forecasts to see if it's a good time for him to act. He doesn't consult human agendas or political offices to see if this would be a good time to demonstrate his power. He doesn't ask about your age or height or experience or education. He opens whatever way he wants, whatever way he wants to.

He is God!

So when you need a way made through something that's beyond your ability, put your faith in God. He split the Red Sea for Israel. He made a highway for them through the desert. He led them into the Promised Land. He fed them with manna from heaven and water from a rock.

If God made a way for Israel through the sea, if he made a way for them through the wilderness, and if he made a way for water to flow through solid rock, he can make a way for you. He can make a way for your business idea to succeed even though you don't have the connections you wish you had. He can make a way past the coldness and distance in your marriage. He can make a way through addiction to a place of peace and self-control. He can make a way through trauma, through betrayal, through divorce, through abuse.

There's a story in Luke 5 about a paralyzed man with four friends who were trying to get to Jesus because they knew Jesus could heal the sick man. The four men couldn't get through the crowd that was gathered around the house Jesus was at, so they climbed on the roof, broke open a hole, and used ropes to lower their friend down at the feet of Jesus. When Jesus saw their faith, he forgave the man's sins and healed him. It's a powerful story of creativity and tenacity. Because they had faith, they found a way past an obstacle, and Jesus did a miracle.

I've had moments like that. I've had miracles like that. I'm sure you have too. In fact, I want you to revisit those memories right now. Think of three things God has done for you when you didn't see a way forward. I want you to remember them right now, before you move on. You had a burst of faith, you worked hard, you took risks, you found a way, and God did the impossible. Those are moments to celebrate. Those are parting-the-Red-Sea miracles when God made a way where there was no way. They are memories to keep at the forefront of your mind when you're going through hard times.

But not every story ends like that. Sometimes the way forward is not what you expected or wanted at all. Sometimes the way takes you through hardship, through heartache, through tragedy. That doesn't mean you didn't have enough faith. If anything, your perseverance in those seasons is the greatest proof of your faith.

There are specific people who come to my mind every time I think about this kind of faith, people who I've watched find a way when the healing didn't come or the miracle wasn't there and the worst thing happened. I think of Tom, for example, a man in my church who started a fishing club called Riley's Catch after his son was killed in a car accident. Riley loved fishing and had planned to start the club before he died. Tom carried out his wish, and hundreds of kids have come to Christ through Riley's Catch. The result doesn't take away Tom's pain or lessen his loss, but he found a way forward, and it was beautiful in its own way.

> The way forward is not an instant miracle that makes everything perfect and pain-free. Rather, it's the presence of divine strength that leads you, tearfully and tentatively, through the tragedy and the heartbreak.

I could list countless others who found a way through impossible pain because they held on to their unbreakable faith. Yes, they walked through a season of mourning. Yes, their hearts were broken. Things were never like they were before. But God, in his perfect time and gentle way, opened up a path of healing and peace for them.

In those moments, the way forward is not an instant miracle that makes everything perfect and pain-free. Rather, it's the presence of divine strength that leads you, tearfully and tentatively, through the tragedy and the heartbreak.

"With God there's always a way" doesn't mean that with God you'll always get *your* way. And that's why you need the second half: "and by *faith* I will find it." You don't need a lot of faith when circumstances go your way. You need faith when they *don't* go your way and you have to believe that this is actually God's way.

Jesus set the example in this. He carried his cross down a road that we call Via Dolorosa—the way of suffering. The night before, he had prayed, "My Father, if it is possible, may this cup be taken from me. Yet not as I will, but as you will" (Matthew 26:39). God didn't take the cup from Jesus. Instead, he took Jesus to the cross.

So when I say that with God there's always a way, I'm not saying with God there's always a way around pain and heartache and tragedy. I'm saying there is always a way *through* whatever God allows you to experience. The Bible says, "Even though I walk through the darkest valley, I will fear no evil, for you are with me" (Psalm 23:4).

Sometimes God takes the thing away, and sometimes he takes you through the thing. Either way, he will be faithful, and he'll keep you safe. And along the way, your faith enables you to grow through whatever you go through.

I remember one video my friend Rick made that discussed many of the failures that led to the season of success he's now experiencing. He went through all the failed bands and all the cross-country tours. He talked about getting dropped from a major record label. He described building a studio in his house only to reach a point where he didn't know how he was going to continue to provide for his family. And yet, through something as small as an offhand suggestion to start a YouTube channel, and through something as consistent as his willingness to bring his full fifty-four-year-old self to the opportunity and to do the work, he has found a way to make a bigger difference than he ever imagined. He now interviews his heroes and touches the lives of millions. God made a way, but it took faith to find it.

Is there something in your life that looks finished, but a voice inside you is telling you that it's not over yet? Is God reminding you, "Go forward! You're not finished"? Listen to that voice. That's the voice of the new you calling you to step into who you really are.

Let faith rise up again. In God, there is a way forward. He is all powerful and always faithful. You might not see the way now, but it will be there when you need it. By faith you will find it, and step by step you'll walk in it.

ELEVEN

NOW MOVE

A while back I was trying to play tennis with one of my best friends, who is a much better tennis player than I am. For some reason, in this particular game, I was up 30-love. I'm sure he was just as shocked as I was.

But he did something that really got my attention. Under his breath he said, "Just beat him back, one ball at a time."

He was coaching himself. Grounding himself. Resetting himself. "Just beat him back, one ball at a time."

And that's what he did. I choked. He won the game, the set, the match. How? By leaving the past behind and just moving forward. I watched him do it. He let go of the frustration, he ignored the mistakes he had made, and he focused on the task at hand: winning the next point. And the next one. And so on until he had completely destroyed my already fragile ego.

I don't know about you, but I get stuck in the past a lot. That dumb thing I said yesterday in a meeting. That moment last night when I snapped at my wife. That comment someone posted online this morning that I can't stop thinking about. That project I was so excited about that ultimately fell through.

It's easy to let things like that lock us into a doom loop of discouragement or self-rejection. But if we just stand there, stuck in guilt or shame or grief or disappointment, we'll end up forfeiting the game.

A mindset that says, "With God there's always a way, and by faith I will find it," doesn't mean you will never make a mistake or feel discouraged. It doesn't mean you'll never miss what you used to have or be nervous about the future. It doesn't mean you will never feel like you're losing the game, the set, the match.

It means that you are willing to leave the past behind and press on toward what lies ahead.

This is often as simple as recognizing that you're not actually stuck in that doom loop. You have a choice. You can decide to get up and get going. Within you lies the power to reset, to shift, to walk toward a better future.

I had a moment just the other day where I was trying to correct one of my kids about something (not napkins) and it got a little more heated than I intended. Correction: *I* got more heated than I intended. It wasn't terrible: I wasn't cussing or slinging plates around the room or anything like that. But it shifted the energy in the room, and I thought, *Oh, man! Now I ruined the whole morning.*

But then I stopped myself. I thought, *You didn't ruin it. Just shift it.*

After about a minute of working through that particular incident, we shifted. We recovered, and the rest of the morning was good.

Do you see how practical this is? How immediate? It's a choice you make to move forward, even in the smallest interactions and decisions.

Victory in life is realized by embracing your capacity to shift, to reset, to embrace what is next.

It happens by taking action: one thought at a time, one prayer at a time, one right choice at a time, one kind word at a time. That's how you beat the enemy back and step into your future.

So ask yourself: "What does moving forward look like in my situation? What is the next thing, the new thing, the *now* thing that I need to do? The next word I speak is going to be positive. The next question I ask is going to be curious, not condemning. The next move I make is going to be one with energy."

> Victory in life is realized by embracing your capacity to shift, to reset, to embrace what is next.

I think sometimes we overestimate the power our past has to hold us back, and we underestimate our freedom to leave those things behind and move forward in faith. We imagine that breaking out of a bad mood, a bad day, or a seemingly unsolvable situation is a major event—but sometimes it's as simple as doing the next right thing.

By "simple," I don't mean to say it's always easy. Life is a lot more complicated than a tennis match. It's simple to tell yourself to put the past behind you and look forward, but sometimes doing the next right thing takes all your focus and energy. Then you have to do it again. And again. And again.

But it is possible.

You can leave the loss, the regret, the guilt behind. You can press on in faith. You can beat the enemy back, one ball at a time.

When Israel reached the border of the Promised Land, while they were in a place called the plains of Moab, God took Moses to the top of a mountain and showed him the land from a distance. The Bible says that after that, Moses died at the age of one hundred and twenty, and God buried him in a place that nobody knew.

Can you imagine how Israel must have felt as they waited at the foot of that mountain? Moses had already told them God wasn't going to let him lead them into the Promised Land, but I'll bet they still had a hard time believing he wasn't returning. After all, he had gone up mountains before and come back, and it was usually for the better. After he climbed Mount Sinai, he came down with his face shining because he had met with God, and he gave them the Ten Commandments.

Israel needed Moses, or so they thought. Sure, they complained about him a lot, but he had been their leader for forty years. Moses was the person who had given them food from heaven and water from a rock. He was the one who spoke to God on their behalf when they had sinned. There was only one Moses. So I'm going to speculate that while they were mourning for Moses, they were also looking for him. I bet they were mobilizing search parties and holding praying vigils because they were hoping to see him come down the mountain one more time.

The Bible says, "The Israelites grieved for Moses in the plains of Moab thirty days, until the time of weeping and mourning was over" (Deuteronomy 34:8). The normal time for grieving in that culture was a week, but Moses was special. He was legendary. So Israel took a whole month to mourn him.

At some point, though, they had to accept the fact that Moses wasn't coming back. Moses was no more.

What now? What next?

It was a moment of decision. The Promised Land was on the horizon. It was in their future, and they were looking forward to it. But in order to step into what was next, they had to leave behind what had happened.

That's not easy. It wasn't easy for them, and it's not easy for us. How long does it take us in seasons of transition to accept that something is never going to be like it once was? Often we keep trying to make things like they were. We get trapped in our memories of the past, reliving something we've lost or had to leave behind, wishing we could go back to those days because they seemed so comfortable, so familiar, so secure.

It's the "good old days" syndrome, where you have an idealized view of the past that keeps you from accepting your present reality and stepping into your future calling. If you're going to follow God's way forward, though, which is the way of faith, sometimes you have to leave Moses on the mountain.

I've been there. In the last few years, I have been reckoning with some realities in my own life that need to be adjusted because things are changing, the world is shifting, and God is moving. If I stay where I am, I will miss what God wants to do in the place he is calling me to.

Letting go of "the good old days" is the first step in moving forward in faith. Israel's story didn't end in the plains of Moab when Moses went missing, and your story isn't over either. Don't let yourself become stuck in a past that is no more. There are good things coming, but you won't experience them if you can't walk toward them.

Sometimes I tell people, don't share your testimony too soon. Don't assume your testimony is complete today, because you might leave out the part God is getting to that you don't know about yet.

> Don't assume your testimony is complete today, because you might leave out the part God is getting to that you don't know about yet.

The uncomfortable seasons we go through are a bit like those videos people post where they have to put "wait for it" or "wait till the end" because they know everyone's attention span is about two seconds long, and they want to make sure they see the good part. Don't give up on your current situation too quickly. Don't call it unimportant, boring, bad, pointless, a waste of time, a loss. Something is ahead. Something is about to happen that you don't see coming.

Wait for it.

There's so much more to your story.

Don't close your heart. Don't close your mind. Don't stop praying. Don't stop believing.

In your life, some of the characters are going to exit. Some conditions are going to change. There will be seasons of loss and grief, but don't let that turn into despair. Don't interpret the death of Moses as the end of a dream. God is making room for what is coming next.

Holly was talking to me the other day about a painful relational change she was going through. Someone who had been her friend for nearly twenty years seemed to be shutting her out of their life, almost overnight. I didn't want to be the stereotypical husband and give her three quick fixes that don't actually fix anything, so I just listened.

Eventually, we came around to this thought. Holly's investment in that friendship wasn't a waste: the relationship had been a gift for almost twenty years. Now, instead of focusing on the loss, she needed to focus on new relationships that had been opening up recently. Moving forward in those relationships wouldn't take the pain away for Holly, of course. But as she began to list new friends God had sent in the same span of time that this older friend had become distant, there was a shift in perspective. The end of the relationship didn't make what she had experienced in the past irrelevant. It was simply a signal that something had shifted. By focusing her attention on the people in her life now, Holly was able to downgrade the disappointment over the friend who had walked away.

I don't want to be the stereotypical pastor, either, and give you five fake fixes for real pain. But I do want to encourage you to evaluate your perspective of the changes or losses you might be experiencing. The pain is real and the grief is valid, but if God allowed something to be taken away from you, he's probably also adding something to you. Do you see any signals that God is doing something different as you move forward?

Deuteronomy says that Israel grieved until "the time of weeping and mourning was over." They spent a month mourning Moses in Moab. Try saying that five times in a row. A *month mourning Moses in Moab.*

It's a lot of *mo's.* And they all ended at once.

"No Mo" is how I think of it. No more Moses. No more mourning a past that will never exist again. No more camping out in Moab hoping for the good old days to return. *No Mo.* The time had come to move forward into the promise of God.

Notice it doesn't say the *feeling* of mourning was over. But the *time* for mourning was over. That isn't meant to be cruel. God isn't saying, "It's over. Get over it. Stop crying. Quit whining. Grow up." And I'm not saying that either. They took a month to mourn because emotions matter.

But eventually, at the right time, mourning needed to give way to movement. They had to go from *No Mo* to *Now Move.*

Your walk with God includes feelings, but your faith is a lot bigger than feelings, and sometimes you have to move forward even when you're still feeling something from the past. You have to move forward even when it still doesn't make sense. You have to move forward when you still have unanswered questions, and some of those questions now have baby questions, and you can't figure any of it out.

Are you in a No Mo season right now? Is it your time to move forward even though you're mourning and missing something you're leaving behind? Have you been holding on to a past that needs to rest in peace on a mountain somewhere? Jesus told one of his disciples, "Follow me, and let the dead bury their own dead" (Matthew 8:22). In other words, don't let what is dead stop you from living.

Maybe it's time to move out of Moab, to stop looking for a Moses who isn't coming back. To stop reliving a season of your life that was awesome but is over now. To quit waiting for someone to apologize for hurting you. To stop fantasizing over a romance that didn't work out. That person already moved to Oklahoma. It's over, and you're still scrolling through Facebook, wondering, "What are they up to now?" Delete the app and live your life. You did what you could. You mourned long enough; now it's time to move forward.

That "month of mourning" is figurative, by the way. If someone put a ding in the door of your brand-new Tesla, you shouldn't need a literal month to grieve. If you lost a loved one, though, you might never "get over" it, and I'm not saying you need to. You'll carry the loss forever, although it won't always hurt as badly as it does now. But you can still move forward when the time is right.

I love the Bible verse that says, "Weeping may stay for the night, but rejoicing comes in the morning" (Psalm 30:5). We're going forward with our tearstained faces, forward with our unanswered questions, forward with our unfinished faith—but forward.

The story doesn't end with the death of Moses, as I said. Right after the mourning period is over, Deuteronomy 34 says, "Now Joshua son of Nun was filled with the spirit of wisdom because Moses had laid his hands on him" (verse 9).

Notice the first two words: "Now Joshua."

God took them from No Mo to Now Joshua. For every No Mo in your life, there is a Now Joshua that God has been developing. For every No Mo you have grieved over, God is saying now move forward into the good gift I have for you.

When you see no more Moses, God says, "Now there's a Joshua." When you see an ending, God is already making a new opening. Where you see no way, God says, "Now, watch me make a way. Let me through. Make some space. Make some room."

Maybe the devil has been telling you, "You're finished. You're done. It's over now." But God says you're not finished because he's not finished. And I think he wants to change that last phrase a little. He wants to put a period in there because punctuation matters. Instead of "It's over now," read it like this: "It's over. Now . . ."

Maybe you've been so caught up in what is gone, what is lost, what is left behind that you can't see how God has been preparing you for what's ahead. You're not finished. You're moving forward. Something is over, but something else is beginning.

What happened is history, but what happens next hinges on how you respond to "now."

You're not just going through a crisis; you're in a cocoon. You're changing in there. You're transforming in there. You're coming out with wings. You're coming out with wisdom. You're coming out with the will of God. Paul wrote, "Forgetting what is behind and straining toward what is ahead, I press on toward the goal to win the prize for which God has called me heavenward in Christ Jesus" (Philippians 3:13–14).

> You're not just going through a crisis; you're in a cocoon. You're changing in there.

What do you need to leave behind so you move forward? What do you need to mourn for a season, then leave buried on a mountain?

You don't dishonor the past by doing that. You aren't being disloyal to the life you're leaving behind. You might think you're being untrue to yourself or to someone else by moving forward, but you can do both. You can miss what you've lost *and* move into what's ahead. You can acknowledge what you've received, you can celebrate how much you've accomplished, you can be grateful for what brought you to this point, *and* choose to leave those things behind and move forward. Don't miss out on Joshua because you're stuck missing Moses.

What is your "Now Joshua"? What doors are opening? What people are coming into your life? What faith is stirring in your heart? What challenges are waiting ahead? What calling has God awakened in your heart?

What is the new thing, the now thing, the next thing that God is doing in you?

Now move.

TWELVE

WEASEL-FREE MENTALITY

I love the book *The Artist's Way* by Julia Cameron. One of the things she writes about is the internal censor or voice that undermines your creativity. She says your censor is the part of yourself that criticizes you and makes fun of you when you start to create. It's the voice that says your work is mediocre and you have no business doing this. It gives you excuses to quit. It pulls you away from the work you're supposed to be doing and into the weeds of self-loathing and premature critique.

I think her point applies to more than just creativity. I think the same dynamic exists in our walk with Jesus as we become who he has called us to be. Walking in the mindset "With God there's always a way, and by faith I will find it" means learning to silence the censor that comes after your creativity, your confidence, and your courage.

Maybe you've experienced this. Maybe you have an internal voice that tries to keep you locked into the old you—the fearful, self-critical, defensive you—instead of allowing you to explore open doors and discover untapped potential. That's the exact opposite of a mindset that focuses on possibility. But when you turn your focus toward God, when you set your mind on the unlimited, unstoppable grace that empowers you to find creative ways forward, the censor loses its leverage.

Julia Cameron suggests finding a cartoon image that represents the censor and putting it somewhere you can see it when you are trying to create. She says, "Just making the Censor into the nasty, clever little character that it is begins to pry loose some of its power over you and your creativity."*

> When you turn your focus toward God, when you set your mind on the unlimited, unstoppable grace that empowers you to find creative ways forward, the censor loses its leverage.

In other words, realizing that there is a difference between the censor and your true, new self is the first act of separation that leads to freedom and flourishing.

When I read that, I decided that I would make my censor a weasel. Why? First, the image fits. Weasels are creepy-looking and destructive. They sneak into gardens and steal the fruit before it's ready to harvest. I think that's the perfect metaphor not only for things that block creativity but also for things that sabotage spiritual growth. When something is growing, it needs to be nurtured, but when we judge it, we interrupt the process. We spoil the fruit before it has a chance to grow into what it could be.

---

* Cameron, Julia. *The Artist's Way: A Spiritual Path to Higher Creativity* (New York: Penguin Group, 2002). Kindle edition (loc. 511).

The second reason I picked a weasel is because of a sermon I preached one time about weasels. You might not have known that the Bible talks about weasels. I didn't either, until I came across a rather obscure passage in Leviticus. Let me give you a quick recap of that sermon because it connects to the mindset we're looking at here.

Leviticus says that the weasel was an unclean animal for the Israelites. That meant they couldn't eat it, which is hard to imagine doing in the first place, but I guess God had to make it clear because some people will eat anything. It also meant that if a weasel died, it would contaminate anything it touched, such as a vessel or clothing. That was the law for all dead animals. The item had to be purified or thrown out.

But there was an exception to the dead-animal rule. The Bible says, "If a carcass falls on any seeds that are to be planted, they remain clean" (11:37).

When I saw that verse hidden in Leviticus, I realized it was a powerful metaphor. Seeds represent possibility. They represent growth and fruit. Sometimes, though, it can seem like a weasel came into your life and dropped dead on top of your seed. It tried to contaminate your dreams, your confidence, your joy, your relationships.

Have you ever felt like there was a dead weasel lying on your seed? Maye it was an unmet expectation. A bad doctor's report. A relapse. A rejection letter. You thought something had potential—and then it seemed to die.

But it's not the *potential* that died. The dream or idea or calling is still there, but there's a weasel on it. You're listening to a censor, a voice, a fear, or a threat that wants you to give up on what God gave you.

I've got good news for you. The seed is still clean. The seed still has life in it. Even if the enemy has made inroads into the garden of your heart and life, even if that weasel has tried to steal what God put there, even if it seems like something died right on top of your dreams, it doesn't kill the seed. The devil can't take from you what God has put in you.

Man, I had fun preaching about that one. The meaning of it has so many manifestations. Seeds are powerful, and their power is in their potential. The seed of an idea, the seed of a thought, the seed of a lyric, the seed of a sermon, the seed of a meeting, the seed of an initiative, the seed of a process, the seed of a collaboration.

You know what is crazy? Sometimes it seems like the enemy believes in our potential more than we do. That's why he sends those little weasels. Weasels of worry. Weasels of inferiority. Weasels that tell you this isn't worth it or you're not worth it. Weasels that say, "This isn't working. That's so stupid. Who do you even think you are to attempt that?" Weasels that die on your seed and make you think the seed itself is dead.

> You have to guard that vulnerable place where you nurture what God is speaking.

But seeds never die.

And weasels always lie.

Don't listen to weasels. Don't let weasels into your process. You have to protect your mind, your emotions, and your decisions from weasels that interrupt what is still growing. You have to guard that vulnerable place where you nurture what God is speaking, or even what you think he *might* be speaking.

Remember, the seed is more powerful than whatever falls on it. You might feel like a dead weasel is on your seed, but that doesn't change the power in your seed. Don't let a dead thing keep the living thing from becoming what it has the ability to be. That "dead thing" might be a failure that still haunts you. It might be critical Instagram comments. It might be no Instagram comments at all when you were sure you'd have dozens. It may go deeper. It may be a loved one you can never please. It may be a betrayal you went through.

I can't tell you what your weasels are, but I can tell you that there is still life in the seed. Go back to the thoughts, ideas, concepts, and relationships that you left on top of the soil of good intentions and never planted because dead things fell on top of them. There is still life there. There is potential in that seed.

The day I named my censor the Weasel, I wrote down on a piece of paper, "Weasel-Free Since 2023." I declared it over my heart. I even ordered two customized aluminum signs, one for me and one for Elijah, to hang up in the places we usually create. They also say "Weasel-Free Since 2023." Of course, they have an image of a weasel with a big line through it. And of course, I might be the most creative dad ever. Or the cheesiest, depending on your taste in home decor. But that sign makes me smile every time I see it. It reminds me that my imagination belongs to God, that my heart is his garden.

On the other hand, sometimes I look at it and think, *That's pretty silly. Nobody knows what that means. What kind of grown man makes signs that say weasel-free?* Notice the irony there. I can be staring at a sign that is meant to criticize my self-critical nature so I can break free from it, but then I start criticizing my critique of my self-criticism. And right now I'm criticizing *that*.

Welcome to weasel world. Welcome to my tormented mind. I'm tormented, but I'm trying.

Keeping a heart weasel-free is hard work, so whenever I have an idea and I hear weasel words, I say—usually silently but sometimes out loud—"Get off my seed, weasel! I know it's just an idea. That's all it's supposed to be. It's just a seed. I don't have to decide what to do with it yet. Maybe I'll forget about it. Maybe I'll hang it on my wall. Maybe I'll tattoo it on my arm. Maybe I'll preach about it. I don't have to judge it yet. I can just enjoy it while it grows."

I want *you* to learn how to enjoy things as they grow. Some of the things that God speaks to you will not be realized in this stage of life. That's okay. Don't let the weasel destroy the potential.

By the way, weasels are not just our inner censors. Even people who mean well can say things that cause us to stop believing in the potential God has put inside of us. An offhand comment like "Huh, that's kind of weird" can become a weasel that gets into our development process and usurps our uniqueness. But people speak from their own perspectives, from their own biases and emotional filters and spiritual templates. Don't let anyone else's limitation become your insecurity.

At the same time, don't be a weasel to other people either. When we're hypercritical of other people's ideas, when we ignore someone's contribution, or when we always interrupt what someone else shares with things that we perceive to be better, we don't give the seed a space to breathe. When we don't give people time to process and nurture something, we're being weasels.

One time, Paul wrote, "I care very little if I am judged by you or by any human court; indeed, I do not even judge myself. My conscience is clear, but that does not make me innocent. It is the Lord who judges me" (1 Corinthians 4:3–4).

In context, Paul was talking about people who criticized his motives and actions. He wasn't saying he never evaluated his way of life—he said he had a clear conscience, so obviously he was doing his best. He was saying he didn't let weasels prematurely interrupt the process. He didn't let censors discourage him. He wasn't going to second-guess everything, defend everything, or attach a disclaimer to everything, just to avoid the possibility of being criticized.

He added, "Therefore judge nothing before the appointed time; wait until the Lord comes. He will bring to light what is hidden in darkness and will expose the motives of the heart. At that time each will receive their praise from God" (verse 5).

God is the judge. He's the only one qualified to know the true nature of anything. I especially love the last phrase there. When God exposes the motives of the heart, we will receive *praise*. That's hard for me to believe. I tend to think that God is going to expose my pride, or my selfishness, or my insecurity, or my short temper.

That's not the nature of God, though. He creates a safe space for you to grow and thrive. He's not like that boss or teacher who delighted in pointing out your mistakes. He's not micromanaging you. He's not censoring your creativity. He's not making fun of your blunders.

He's looking for reasons to praise you.

And he finds them everywhere.

One of the things I've been learning lately is how to respect and protect the living seed of what God speaks to me. I'm learning to give myself permission to process my ideas rather than interrupting my assessment of the value of something because of a criticism, a doubt, or a sideways comment from someone.

That means I'm going to scribble ideas down when I have them, even if they seem silly and I don't plan to show anybody. That means I'm going to sing into my phone and mumble ideas unapologetically because I don't get charged by the minute for recording voice memos. That means if I feel like I'm supposed to share something that's a little rough around the edges with a friend to encourage them, I'm going to do that. That means if I'm in a collaborative creative session and I have an idea that is unpolished but has potential, I'm going to put it out there, just in case, even if I feel a little stupid while I do it. That means I'm going to show up for the important moments in my kids' lives, even if I don't have it all together when I do. That means I'm going to lean into opportunities for love, knowing that they will be messy and imperfect.

> Remember, with God there is always a way, and by *faith* you will find it, not by self-doubt or self-ridicule.

As for me and my house, we will be weasel-free. I want to create an atmosphere for my kids where they know it's okay to create something just for the joy of creating it. If it's not hurting anybody, and if they're not making meth, go ahead! Be creative. Make something, say something, do something. I want to be the kind of person who doesn't squelch what somebody else is working on or working through, but rather gives them space to see what their seed can be.

How about you? What seeds do you need to redeem? What dreams do you need to reconvene with in this season of your life? Remember, with God there is always a way, and by *faith* you will find it, not by self-doubt or self-ridicule. Not by asking the opinion of weasels. Not by letting your inner censor bully you into blandness. Not by sitting on seeds that are meant to be planted. You find your way forward by ignoring the inner critic and sowing your seeds in faith.

You never know what the seed will produce until you plant it, and you can't plant it until you get the weasel off of it. Declare your heart weasel-free and see what your seed can be.

THIRTEEN

WHAT IF THIS SUCCEEDS?

The other day I came across a demo version of a song I had written a long time ago. I played it for Holly. It was about ten years old, and it was cringe-inducing, to say the least. I was laughing out loud as we listened because I couldn't believe we had even thought it was worth recording at the time.

I watched Holly's face, and she looked confused and a little annoyed. Finally, she said, "Why are you playing this?" It was her polite way of begging me to turn it off.

But then, about two minutes in, we came to one line that she recognized, and her facial expression changed. You see, even though most of that song ended up on the cutting room floor, there were a few lines that went on to become part of another song that we still sing today, years later. In fact, it's one of the most well-loved songs our church has ever released. It turned out that even in a bad song, there were good lines.

I remember all the writing sessions around that first track. We tried time after time to make it work, to force it to take shape. And every time, we failed. It was frustrating. But eventually, those failed attempts produced a beautiful thing that continues to encourage people and point them to God. Buried within something bad were the seeds of something special.

Why do I share this? Because this is true in many areas of our lives. Often the seed of tomorrow's success is hidden within today's failure.

> **Often the seed of tomorrow's success is hidden within today's failure.**

Great things rarely come easily. They hardly ever happen on the first try. That's the unsexy truth of the creative process, and it's the reality of life in general. It's true whether you're trying to start a business, learn a sport, take up a hobby, record an album, write a children's book, become an influencer, invent new technology, or anything else that stretches you beyond your current capacity.

Tom Waits, the famous singer and songwriter, once said in an interview, "Some songs don't want to be recorded. You can't wrestle with them or you'll only scare them off more. Trying to capture them is trying to trap birds. Some songs come easy like digging potatoes out of the ground or like gum found under an old table. Some songs are only good to cut up as bait and use to catch other songs."[*]

I love the imagery there, and I think it applies to more than just songwriting. The complexity and frustration he expressed are relatable to anybody. Growth isn't a linear

---

[*] Reysean Williams, "Why Do People Like Tom Waits?" *Rawkus Magazine* (February 9, 2016), https://www.rawckus.com/why-do-people-like-tom-waits.

process. You don't always go from one successful version of yourself to the next or from one victorious event to another. Often, like Tom Waits says about those songs that are only good for bait, you have to repurpose pieces of your failure to frame your future.

Remember, the new-you mentality says, "With God there's always a way, and by faith I will find it." Exploring possibilities and knocking on doors can feel complex and frustrating. That doesn't mean you're doing it wrong, though. That's what you have to remind yourself. You're trying something new, you're building something step by step, and that is going to feel messy.

At first, that thing you are doing—like the song I played for Holly—might seem to suck. You might say, "Why am I here? Why am I doing this? What is the point of all this? This is embarrassing." But maybe what you think sucks is actually a seed. Maybe your future will be found in your frustration. Maybe it will flow from your failures. Maybe your first drafts, your first steps, your first attempts will set something in motion that God will make beautiful in his time.

Instead of getting depressed over the inevitable mistakes along the way, why not focus on the possibilities ahead? Why not dream about what could happen? Imagine the people you could impact. Imagine the legacy you could leave. Imagine the quality of life you could enjoy and the satisfaction you could experience.

I came across a scripture several years ago that talks about this, and I've gotten obsessed with it. I find it to be mysterious, and yet in its mystery, it's clarifying. "Sow your seed in the morning, and at evening let your hands not be idle, for you do not know which will succeed, whether this or that, or whether both will do equally well" (Ecclesiastes 11:6).

Often, I think we don't initiate the things we hold in our hearts because we're intimidated by this fear-infusing question: *What if it fails?* Someone once suggested to me, "Why don't you flip the question? Say to yourself, *What if it works?*" It sounds simple, but to make that switch changes everything.

That's what Solomon is saying in this verse. "Flip the question! Don't just sit around wondering if your ideas might work or not. Try this and try that, because maybe one will succeed, or maybe both will succeed. But you won't know until you try. So sow your seed!"

The old you might have said, "What if this crashes and burns? I'd better not even try. Or if I do try, I'm going to aim low. I'm going to expect the worst. I'm going to quit at the first sign of resistance." That version of you might have made excuses, led with disclaimers, and written a resignation speech before failure had even happened. "The economy is bad, so this probably won't work. There's too much competition, so I doubt I'll succeed. I'm going to try, but I'm not getting my hopes up."

But that's the not you God sees. That's not the knew you—the new you. The authentic, faith-filled, possibility-focused you doesn't ask, "What if this fails?" but rather, "What if this succeeds?" Why not start from *that* mentality, rather than assuming the worst? Why not aim high and risk disappointment, rather than aiming low and guaranteeing a life filled with *what ifs*? Instead of predicting your own failure, say, "What if this succeeds beyond my wildest dreams? What if this turns into something I love? What if God plans to take this places I never expected?"

I wrote something down on a sticky note recently. By the way, I have sticky notes all over my house to keep myself on track because I need the reminders. On this one, I wrote, "The oh-so-sad but not-so-surprising statistics of unsown seeds. One hundred percent of unsown seeds fail to sprout and grow."

The point I was making to myself was that seeds that are never sown will never succeed. They have a 100 percent failure rate. The seeds of the words we didn't speak. The

> Seeds that are never sown will never succeed.

seeds of the yeses we couldn't quite commit to. The seeds of the dreams we never dared to verbalize. The seeds of the invitations for collaboration that we never extended because they might end in rejection.

The unsurprising statistic of unsown seeds is that every seed you keep in your bag and don't put in the soil of real life will stay dormant. It is potential untapped. It is fruit unrealized. You're carrying something: a gift, a talent, an idea, a mission, a purpose, a calling. You have to sow your seed so that it has a chance to succeed.

But what if it sucks?

It's a fear we all face. So let me encourage you. *It will suck.* At least for a little while. Everything goes through a stage where it's not very good. In writing, it's called a rough draft. In product development, it's called a prototype. In film, it's called a storyboard. In art, it's called a sketch. In technology, it's called a minimum viable product.

It's not pretty. It's not polished. It's a barebones version of something that will exist, but some bugs have to be worked out first. That will take time, and it will go through a lot of iterations along the way.

You have to get through each stage of growth or you'll never get to where God is taking you. But if you're so afraid of looking stupid or making mistakes that you aren't willing to put an imperfect version of yourself out there and fix the flaws that appear, you'll fail by default.

I was in a meeting recently, and someone made a statement that stuck with me. She said, "I'm going to dare to suck right now." I liked the phrase. She was giving herself permission to be imperfect as we discussed the ideas that were on the table. Permission to try, to explore, to make a first-draft fool of herself, to learn, to grow.

The word "dare" was a good term because real risk is involved, so real courage is needed. When you try new things, when you commit to growth, you're signing up for a messy process. You might fail spectacularly. You might get laughed at. You might have to apologize. You might lose some money. You might waste some time.

Get used to that.

It's called growth. It's called humility. It's called humanity. It's called making peace with your imperfections because perfection is impossible and overrated anyway, but *becoming a fuller version of you* is beautiful.

I'm not minimizing the pain inherent in the process. I'm just saying you shouldn't make the pain worse by expecting perfection on the first try. Set the bar high, but don't expect to clear it on the first jump. You have to work up to it.

Even if what you try is really bad at first, you might find some seeds in it. You'll get through the initial stage and say, "Well, all of *that* was bad, but *this* right here, this is good." If you move toward what you think God has called you to do and then realize it's not the right direction, within that failure you might find the core of the thing that you were actually called to.

I'm not saying that mistakes are no big deal. I hate them. I'm a perfectionist by nature, so I have to continually talk myself through this principle I'm sharing right now. Working on the same song in multiple writing sessions only to end up throwing it out was frustrating, not fun. It made me feel like a failure and a hack. In the moment, anyway. But when I hear the song that came from it, I don't think about the pain of the process. I don't remember the suffering in the sowing.

What I feel is the joy of harvest.

Psalms says, "Those who sow with tears will reap with songs of joy. Those who go out weeping, carrying seed to sow, will return with songs of joy, carrying sheaves with them" (126:5–6). A focus on possibility means that you keep your eyes on the hope set before you, not on every little mistake you make along the way.

This isn't denial; it's expectation. It's faith. It's knowing that in God you will find a way forward. It might take a while, and you might have a few false starts and run into a few dead ends, but that's okay. You have to go through it to get to the benefit on the other side.

One thing I have grown to love—very unexpectedly—is cold plunging. A friend of mine got me to try it a few years ago at a hotel. In case you've never heard of this voluntary form of self-torture, a cold plunge is when you immerse your-self in ice water for a short time because it's supposed to pro-mote blood circulation, reduce inflammation, and improve mental alertness.

The first time I did it, I stayed in the water for exactly the one minute we had agreed on, then I jumped out and ran to the nearest available sauna. Now, I have to make myself get out of a cold plunge after ten minutes. I learned this the hard way after staying in a little too long one time and being unable to feel my toes or even walk for fifteen minutes. I'm a little bit of an extremist, apparently.

When you first get in that ice-cold water, all you're think-ing is, *Why did I voluntarily do this to myself? I'm freezing.* For the first forty-five seconds, that's what fills your mind. *I'm an idiot. I never should have watched that interview with Wim Hof, the Iceman. I want to die right now.*

Then you start to settle. You shiver, but you settle. And for me, I feel really good afterward. Going through the dis-comfort gets me to a place where I get the benefits.

When it comes to stepping into new things, I think a lot of us never get to the settling because we are afraid of the shiver-ing. We don't plant the seeds because we don't dare to suck. And I get it. I do the same thing sometimes because the uncer-tainty of not knowing what will happen is scary. What if it doesn't work? What if they don't like it? What if they reject it?

Well . . . what if? Play the thought out. Will they remember your failure forever? Will your reputation be ruined beyond repair? I mean, what's the worst thing that could happen?

I remember listening to a sermon by a pastor I respected years ago. I was sitting in an arena packed with thirty thou-sand people. The sermon wasn't his finest. Actually, to be totally candid, he bombed. Then the service ended, and I went out for lunch. So did everyone else.

That was it.

I didn't think less of him after that. I haven't spent the last thirteen years mocking him in my mind. I just assumed he had an off day or that I wasn't in the right headspace myself, and I ate my hamburger steak and drank my Diet Coke.

In a morbid kind of way, that experience actually encouraged me because when you're onstage and it's not going very well, you feel like it's the end of the world. You have to remind yourself that the people in the audience might be nicer to you than you are, and they aren't as invested in this as you are. They're listening, but they're also thinking, *Chipotle or Chick-fil-A? What do I feel like today?*

I'm not saying that preaching isn't important or that the quality of your work doesn't matter. I'm just saying that messing up isn't as big of a deal as the enemy wants you to think. Most people are too busy dealing with their own battles and thinking about their own needs to spend a lot of energy judging you for yours. Plus, many of them are better at showing compassion and mercy to you than you are.

> God is a safe place for you to try and fail.

And so is God.

God is a safe place for you to try and fail. If you sink when you try walking on water, it's not as big of a problem as you think because Jesus will bring you back to the boat. Remember, Jesus helped Peter grow in faith through that experience. When it was all over and Jesus had stilled the storm, Peter and all the disciples realized, "You really are the Son of God." The seeds of that revelation were sown in Peter's failure.

Here's the principle: God shows up when you slip up.

A lot of us want to live an error-free life, but how can you expect God to show up if you aren't willing to slip up? The cycle of godly success is this: you step up, you slip up, and God shows up. Then you step up again, you slip up again, and God shows up again. And through it all, you grow into the person God knew you would be.

Solomon said, "You do not know which will succeed, whether *this* or *that*, or whether both will do equally well." In order to let the seed grow, you have to let go of your need for certainty. You have to be okay with not knowing whether this will work or not. *This* might succeed, or *that* might, or both might. But you won't know if you don't sow.

You know what this means? Since we can't predict what will succeed, we need a lot of "thises" and "thats" in our lives. Sometimes a *that* will come back to you, and you'll say, "Wow, *that* person is now a part of my life? *That* project worked out? *That* person became a client? *That* conversation with my kid was the one that changed things? *That* job application put my career on track? *That*? Oh, okay. Well, let me get busy with another *this*."

That's what Solomon is saying. Get busy with a this so you can look back at a that. Someday you'll say, "I'm glad I did that. I'm glad I said that. I'm glad I pushed through that. I'm glad I booked that. I'm glad I tried that. I'm glad I apologized for that. I'm glad I asked for that."

What seed do you have today? Sow *this* so *that* can happen. "Sow this, so that." It's catchy when you say it out loud. It means there is purpose in my work because there is potential in my seed.

To sow in the morning and not be idle in the evening does not mean you work twelve-hour days and never show up for your family, or that you refuse to stop and appreciate how far you've come. It doesn't mean you blow up your marriage or ruin your health because you're so stressed out all the time. It's a metaphor. It means you don't let your hands be still when they should be busy. The work of sowing includes so much more than your day job too. It includes your dreams. Your family. Your health. Your walk with God. Your calling.

Don't let your hands be idle when there's work to do. Invest in what will bring a return not just financially, but relationally and emotionally and spiritually. Sow these things now so that you'll reap a return later.

That's the sowing cycle. While you're sowing this, you're reaping that; while you're planting that, you're harvesting this. In times of abundance, don't get so distracted with your reaping that you forget to sow for tomorrow. And in times of waiting, don't get so hyperfocused on sowing that you forget to be grateful for the harvests you've had and the ones that are coming.

You should always be sowing something now so you'll have something to reap later. If it doesn't work out, take the seed from the failure and sow it back into the soil of your faith. Give God the mistakes of today and ask him to make them wisdom for your future. And if it does work out, if you do succeed, sow your successes back in by giving praise to God. Turn it into gratitude.

Whatever point of the cycle you're in right now—whether it's the dream, the disappointment, or the wonderful stage called delivery—keep sowing. Keep going. Keep pressing. Use the momentum.

You might deal with some doubts along the way. The weasel may try to tell you that you look stupid, that you're not helping anybody, that you don't know what you're doing. You might hear a voice whisper in your head, "What if this fails?"

> Give God the mistakes of today and ask him to make them wisdom for your future.

Flip the question and whisper back, "But what if it *succeeds*? I'm not stopping. I'm not idle. I'm focusing on possibilities, and I'm looking forward to what God has for me. With God there is always a way, and by faith I will find it."

I love how this mindset starts and ends with God, not just with us. *He* makes the difference. *He* makes us strong. *He* makes a way. God's faithfulness is always the foundation of our faith.

That's essential because when life gets difficult, it's easy to feel like you have to face everything on your own, like you're trying to navigate a deep, dark forest and all you have is an iPhone flashlight. You can feel overwhelmed by the weight of it all, scared that if you fall or if you fail, you'll let everybody down.

You might even feel like you're letting *God* down. I know I do sometimes. I can project my own insecurities onto God, and I start to wonder if maybe I'm on his last nerve, and he's running out of patience with me.

Maybe you do the same thing. I think we all do at times. That's why I love this next mindset so much. Don't tell the other mindsets, but I think it's my favorite. It goes like this: *God is not against me, but he's in it with me, working through me, fighting for me.*

GOD IS NOT AGAINST ME, BUT HE'S IN IT WITH ME, WORKING THROUGH ME, FIGHTING FOR ME.

ACTION STEP:
WALK IN CONFIDENCE.

FOURTEEN

THAT LIZARD IS LOUD

A few years ago, my daughter, Abbey, had just learned to swim underwater, and she wanted to show her brothers she could cross the pool in one breath. She was only seven, and they couldn't cross it in one breath until they were maybe ten, so she wanted everybody to see what she could do.

But she had never done it before. So I told her, "All right. We can do this. Just remember, the lizard brain is going to be telling you that you can't do it. But the lizard is lying."

She said, "Wait. There's a lizard in my brain?"

I said, "No, baby. It's just that the human brain . . ." And then I tried to explain to a seven-year-old about the survival part of our brain, the fight-or-flight part that kicks in when we are in an emergency. When we are scared for our lives, our brains don't process at the level of wisdom but rather at the level of fear. I told her some people call this the lizard brain.

Now, between the weasel-free mentality we talked about earlier and the lizard brain, you might thing I have a strange obsession with critters. I don't. I just like metaphors. And by the way, the science behind the lizard brain theory has been debunked now. I'm a pastor, though, not a psychologist, and at the time, "lizard brain" was a pretty good label for a little girl to understand irrational fear. Since she was seven, she believed me, which is what little kids do. Then they become teenagers and think you're an idiot every time you open your mouth. But that's another topic.

Anyway, I told her, "Don't listen to the lizard. You're going to go under the water, and you're going to think you're about to die, but you're not going to die. Just don't listen to the lizard."

She went underwater, swam clear to the other end, and came up gasping but smiling. She was so proud.

I yelled, "Amazing! You did it! How did you feel?"

She said, "Man, that lizard is loud!"

I asked, "What did you say back to him?"

She yelled back, "I told him, 'Shut up, lizard! I'm doing this.'"

I loved that response. I use it myself sometimes now: "Shut up, fear! Shut up, insecurity! Shut up, worry! I'm doing this. I don't have to listen to you. I'm not going to die. I'm not going to fall apart. I'm moving forward, and you can't stop me."

Are there any areas of your life where you've been listening to the lizard? Where fear has started to take on a voice of its own, and it's telling you that you're going down, you're about to drown, you'll never make it to the other side? Remember, the lizard is a liar.

A lizard brain is the old version you. The new you says, "Shut up, fear! I'm doing this! I am going to make it. I'm going to live and not die. I'm going to raise my kids. I'm going to make a difference in the world. I'm going to get out of this hole I'm in. I'm going to reach the goal I set. I'm taking my thoughts back. I'm getting my confidence back."

I'm sure you've noticed that your mind can escalate things very quickly. In a split second, your emotions can paint a worst-case picture of the future, and your thoughts can go to a dark place, a place that often isn't even real. Then fear and discouragement transport you back to a lesser version of yourself, and you start reacting and responding because you're triggered by trauma. You might be shrinking back from things that aren't even in your life anymore or because you are imagining forty-seven terrible, hypothetical scenarios.

Sometimes those thoughts are just your brain helping you plan for contingencies, but other times they are the lizard lying to you again. It's the old you trying to stage a comeback. You have to learn what that voice sounds like and politely tell it to shut up, because it's not the voice of God and it doesn't represent what he thinks about you or says about you.

So how do you overcome these thoughts of fear, failure, and worst-case scenarios? Of impending doom and imminent loss?

First, you recognize the lizard voice for what it is: your fight-or-flight instinct spiraling out of control.

Second, you give your mind something healthier to hold on to. That's where this mindset comes in. Earlier, I called it my favorite mindset. It holds a lot of personal meaning for me. Say it loud, if you can: *God is not against me, but he's in it with me, working through me, fighting for me.*

You have to trust that God wants to work with you. If you don't, how could you possibly be a good parent? How could you run a business? How could you graduate from school or get your master's degree or fight diabetes or continue to show up and see your mom at the nursing home when she doesn't even know who you are? How could you push through that kind of opposition if you don't believe God is with you and for you?

I love every part of this affirmation. "God is not against me" means that he's not out to get me. He's not mad at me for my mistakes. He's not frustrated with my frailty or caught off guard by my failure.

"He's in it with me" means we're doing this together. He's not going to abandon me. He's close to me no matter what I'm going through.

"Working through me" means the power comes from him, but I have a part to play. I do what I do by the strength of God at work in me.

> No one can curse what God has blessed. He's a defender of the weak, and he's fighting on my behalf.

And the last phrase, "Fighting for me," means that at the end of the day, the battle belongs to the Lord. God has my back. No one can curse what God has blessed. He's a defender of the weak, and he's fighting on my behalf.

God is not against me, but he's in it with me, working through me, fighting for me. Repeat it to yourself. It's easy to remember, and easy is what you need when the lizard gets loud.

When you have to talk yourself down off a ledge, when you have to walk yourself through overwhelming emotions and the negative thoughts that seem to come out of nowhere, you have to change the way you think, and that starts with changing the way you speak to your situation. Say to your fear of failure, "God is not against me. He's on my side." Say to the panic and terror that come in the middle of the night, "God is not against me. He's working through me." Say to the negative, pessimistic thoughts, "God is not against me. He's fighting for me."

The story of Gideon in Judges 6 is a good example of a lizard-level reaction. When the story opens, Gideon was threshing wheat in a winepress because he was hiding his harvest from the Midianites, an enemy nation who had been oppressing Israel for years.

A winepress was a hidden place. A low place. A small, closed-in space. I wonder, how often do we hide what God has given us in a small place? Inside a closed-in, limited mentality?

When we get scared, we tend to shrink ourselves. We start running from stuff and hiding from stuff, even if nothing is chasing us, and even when God has made us strong enough for the challenge at hand.

I've done that before. You probably have too. And then you wonder, *Why am I down here in this winepress threshing my wheat? Why do I live with such a defensive mentality? Why am I playing not to lose, rather than playing to win?*

Well, it's because you've been attacked before. It's because you've been rejected before. It's because you've tried to step into something greater before. Then you look at what's ahead of you in this season of your life, and you think, "I'm not enough for this. I'm not as smart as them. I'm not as good as them."

Shrinking feels safer, but it's not. Gideon was trying to keep his wheat from the Midianites, but there was no guarantee he was safe down there. And while he was trying to protect the little he had, the entire land was under siege.

He was in survival mode, in fight-or-flight mode. But that's meant to be a temporary setting, not a permanent condition. There will be seasons when all your energy has to go to survival. Maybe your wife is in the hospital and you're juggling work and bills and kids and fear. Maybe you're a new parent and you're living on three hours of sleep a night, and you're dragging your zombie self to the office every day. That's understandable. There's grace for that. Do what you need to do to get through.

But *staying* in survival mode? *Living* in survival mode? Shrinking yourself and hiding yourself as a way of life? That's not God's intention for you.

I have a friend who is a former UFC champion. He told me something he would say to himself before going into a fight: "Survive the assault, work the cut." *Survive the assault* means that when the opponent comes at you furiously and you're taking a beating, the only goal is to survive. Don't get knocked out or choked out in that round.

The second half, *work the cut*, is about offense. It means focusing on the area where the opponent is weak, the place they've taken some damage. You don't try to knock them out with every punch, but instead you just keep breaking them down, one blow at a time. After the assault, there will be a moment to go on offense, to make impact, to connect. That's when you work the cut.

When the angel of the Lord came to Gideon, the first thing he said was, "The LORD is with you, mighty warrior" (Judges 6:12). He was saying, "Gideon, you're a great warrior, and you survived the assault. Now it's time to work the cut."

But Gideon was stuck in survival mode so he skipped over the compliment God was giving him and brought up a complaint: "If the LORD is with us, why has all this happened to us?" (verse 13). His logic was that God couldn't possibly be with them because they were facing too much opposition.

Do you ever let your complaints cancel out God's compliments? I do. I can have my mind so focused on what is missing or broken in me that when God tries to tell me what I am capable of, I downplay the opportunity and exaggerate the obstacles.

God told Gideon, "Go in the strength you have and save Israel out of Midian's hand. Am I not sending you?" (verse 14). Then Gideon pushed back again. "But how can I save Israel? My clan is the weakest in Manasseh, and I am the least in my family" (verse 15).

Can you hear echoes of a lizard in there? Can you see how Gideon was talking himself out of his calling by pointing to his past experience and his present environment?

I don't blame him. I've been stuck in lizard land before. I've had seasons of assault that lasted so long I almost forgot the time to work the cut was coming.

Maybe you've been there too. You might be there right now. It's difficult to see the strength within you if you are trapped in a winepress of fear, depression, anxiety, or lack. When you are more aware of the enemies who are after you than the strength that is inside you, it's hard to have faith for great things.

God wants to speak to you in the winepress, though, just like he did for Gideon. I believe God wants to show you what he's preparing for you. I believe he wants to meet with you wherever you're at and give you a renewed sense of hope and mission. I think he wants you to see the door of opportunity he is offering you.

But it's not just God giving you the opportunity. God is asking *you* to give you the opportunity. What will you do with what he's asking of you? Will you listen to his voice—or to the voice of catastrophe, of calamity, of worst-case scenarios? Will you believe the lizard or will you believe the Lord?

I wish I could say that I always get this right, but I don't. That's exactly why this mindset is my favorite. I remind myself on a regular basis that God is not against me, but he's in it with me, working through me, fighting for me.

How many times have I had God tell me something in his Word, through his Spirit, or through someone else he wanted to use to encourage me, but I couldn't receive it because I was hiding in a winepress? Because I was overwhelmed by opposition? Because I had adopted a victim mentality? Because I saw myself as weak, least, and last?

Sometimes we get the enemy wrong. We think *we're* the enemy: all of the weaknesses in our lives, all of the things that are wrong with us. We're embarrassed by them. We think they have to change before God can use us. "I need to fix this. I need to fix that. Then I can do what God is asking me to do." If your approach to life is always, "What's wrong with me? Where am I off? What do I have to fix before I can be worthy of doing something for God?" it will flood you so fast you won't even be able to focus on what's next. But you will never get to your breakthrough by following the path of blame.

Let me tell you something I believe with all of my heart. There is nothing wrong with you that can't be worked through. God's calling isn't based on your resources or résumé, but on his knowledge and power.

Remember, Gideon was hiding when God said, "You are a mighty warrior!" He was whining in a winepress when God said, "Go in the strength you have." His family and neighbors were worshipping false gods when the true God showed up. Gideon was not a clear choice for a hero commission. Not by a long shot. But God chose him even though he wouldn't have chosen himself.

He does the same with you and me.

God never confuses who you are with where you're at. You can be in a horrible divorce, but God doesn't see you as being incapable of love. You can be in a terrible funk, but God doesn't see you as being incapable of joy. You could be in an impossible financial situation, but God doesn't see you as incapable of providing. He doesn't see you according to the state you're in but according to the strength he has given you.

> God's calling isn't based on your resources or résumé, but on his knowledge and power.

Somebody told me recently that if I could see me like they see me, I wouldn't be so hard on myself. I asked what they meant, and they said, "I see you through eyes of love." I wondered, *If they see me through eyes of love, and if God sees me through eyes of love, shouldn't I see myself through eyes of love?* The lens I look at myself through is often not one of love, but of limitation or even self-loathing. Why? Because I know myself all too well.

Or do I?

Do I know the me I've seen up until now, or do I know the real me? Do I know the miserable me or the mighty me? The whining me or the warrior me? The hidden, hesitant me or the go-in-the-strength-God-gave-me me?

When you seek God, he reveals himself to you. But that's not all he does. As he reveals himself to you, he also reveals *you* to you. Not the old you, not the you you've always known, but the version of you he sees. Then he speaks to your true self, "You're a mighty warrior. I see you that way. I made you that way. I put a lot of things in you that you haven't seen yet because you've been hiding from them, but you're about to discover them as you do what I'm calling you to do. Now go in the strength you have."

God has spoken it. You've got to *go*, though. To discover your strength, you have to move forward in response to what God has said. That's where the discovery happens. What other option is there? Hide your strengths? Bury your gifts? Deny the true reason you're alive?

A while back, my son Elijah was playing *Fortnight*, and I heard him yelling into his headset. "Bro, stop camping. Stop camping! Come on, man, that's lame!" I asked him why he was yelling, and he told me a camper is someone who doesn't really play the game; they just hide out and snipe from a distance. They don't engage, don't take a risk, don't play up to their potential.

I wonder, how often does God come calling only to find me camping? Am I content to stay huddled over my harvest, trying to keep my stuff from getting stolen? To take a few shots from a distance but never get in the game, never take a risk, never engage to the level of my potential?

Remember, it's harder for the enemy to hit a moving target. Read that again. *It's harder for the enemy to hit a moving target.* Often the answer to the fear you feel isn't to stay still but to get going.

God was telling Gideon, "Get going. Be a moving target. If the enemy is going to come after you, don't let him find you in the winepress. Let him find you on the field of battle, and then watch what I do through you."

I want you to say this out loud: "It may end in failure, but I will not live in fear." That phrase got deep in me one day when I said it to myself, because I found myself wanting to hide. Specifically, I was thinking about how many of my friends had recently experienced painful seasons of failure. My initial instinct was to think, *Well what's the point? So many people fail and fall apart. Why even try?*

Rather than denying the possibility of failure, though, I decided to embrace it so God can empower me through it. It may end in failure, but I will not live in fear. I know it sounds a little negative on the surface.

> It may end in failure, but I will not live in fear.

I don't mean that I am a failure or that I expect to fail. I just mean that I don't know how my story is going to go. No one does.

I'm sure I'll fail more than a few times, but I'm not going to live scared. I'm not going to prepay the price of failure by withdrawing into a winepress. If I do take some damage, I want to fail while I'm fighting, not get hit while I'm hiding.

I don't know if I'm going to win great victories in every season. I don't know if I'm going to climb up or fall down in any given endeavor. You don't know either. I'm sure there will be a balance of both for all of us. But if God is with us, we have to walk out of the winepress. We won't find out until we step out. If we're going to get attacked by the enemy, let it happen while we're moving toward something that's worth attaining.

Haters are gonna hate. Critics are gonna criticize. Critters are gonna crit. Lizards are gonna lie. That's what they do. But you don't have to listen to them. They can't overrule what God says about you. For fear to shut up, you have to step up.

If God is for you, no demon or devil, lie or lizard, or fear or foe can ultimately prevail against you. He's on your side. He's got your back. He's in it with you, working through you, fighting for you.

FIFTEEN

DON'T SAY THAT

My children have a problem with closing doors. I cannot explain it; I can only observe it. And complain about it. And resent it. Cupboard doors, pantry doors, the front door, the back door, the garage door—they stay open until I stomp by and shut them.

I hear my mom's voice in my head whenever I see one of the doors to the house left open. "Shut the door!" she would yell when we were kids. "Are you trying to cool off the whole neighborhood? You're letting the cold air out, and you're letting the flies in."

I was walking through our house the other day, closing one door after another. As we've already established, I can be a bit petty. While I was slamming doors shut, I was giving a little speech under my breath. "This is fine. I'll just be the official door closer around here. I've got nothing better to do. It's not like I work all day or anything. I love to follow y'all around and close all the doors so the dumb dog y'all made me buy doesn't get out and get hit by a car. That's exactly what I planned to do today: just close all the doors behind you."

Suddenly a thought went through my mind. Maybe it was God speaking. Maybe it was just my better nature. "I wonder what would happen if I were this concerned about what I let into my heart? What if I were this worked up over what I let out of my mouth? I'm so worried about letting flies in, but I let fear in. I'm so worried about letting the cool air out, but I let negativity, gossip, and anger out."

I didn't stop being irritated, and I still kept slamming doors shut a little harder than I needed to, but it did make me think. I remembered the verse that says, "Above all else, guard your heart, for everything you do flows from it" (Proverbs 4:23).

If we aren't careful, we can let all kinds of things get into our hearts. We can let bad news take us into a spiral of doom and despair. We can let a minor setback in how we planned our day throw us into a state of emotional urgency. We can let a slight offense turn into a feeling of total rejection.

With just a thought or two, we let faith leak out and we let fear come in. We lose our confidence because we lose control of our internal confession.

Now, I'm not saying to lie about what is happening around you. I'm not saying to pretend everything is fine if it's not. What I'm saying is, don't leave the door wide open to negativity and doubt. When bad news comes, tell yourself, "Yes, this is bad. Yes, this sucks. But God is in it with me. He's still working through me, and he's going to fight for me."

When God called Jeremiah to be a prophet, Jeremiah didn't believe he was capable of stepping into God's destiny.

He was too discouraged by his pessimistic self-assessment to trust God's vision for him. So he said, "Alas, Sovereign LORD, I do not know how to speak; I am too young" (Jeremiah 1:6).

I'm sure that if you have small kids (or teenagers, actually), you've heard responses like this a thousand times. "I can't. It's too hard. I don't know how. I'm too little." Kids can build entire worlds online but they can't figure out how to mop the floor. They know the backstory of every Marvel superhero but forget where the garbage bags are stored in the pantry. And they are incapable of closing doors. It's unbelievable.

As a parent, you understand that their "reasons" are really just excuses to quit too easily. So you say to them, "Yes, you can do it. Here, I'll show you how for the twentieth time. Then you're going to do what I know you're capable of doing." Or sometimes you just take out the trash yourself because it's easier.

When it comes to Jeremiah, I don't blame him for making excuses. I'm sure he was scared of the calling God had for him. But his arguments were a smokescreen that stopped him from seeing his true self. They were a cage that kept him from his calling.

God said to Jeremiah, "Do not say, 'I am too young.' You must go to everyone I send you to and say whatever I command you. Do not be afraid of them, for I am with you and will rescue you" (verses 7–8). Jeremiah believed his own excuses, but God saw past them, just like he does when we try to deny who we really are.

A friend of mine named Brendon Burchard, a leading personal development coach, says there are three main excuses we make for not stepping into our potential:

"I don't have it."

"I don't know how."

"I'm not like them."

Jeremiah's arguments fit into all three of those categories. "I don't have the skill. I don't have the clout. I don't know how to speak well. I'm not like those other prophets, the 'real' prophets people would respect. I'm too young and inexperienced." He assumed his own failure so he wouldn't have to risk actually experiencing it.

Do you ever do that? I do. About five times a day. On a good day. No sooner does a good idea pop into my head than four other thoughts appear to tell me why it won't work and how unqualified I am to carry it out anyway.

I find myself using these three phrases far more often than I should, and I wonder if you might too. They don't sound like excuses when you say them—they sound like logic. At least to you and me. But God knows they are excuses. And he says, "Yes, you can do it. Here, I'll show you how for the twentieth time. Then you're going to do what I know you're capable of doing."

Because these excuses are so common and so subtle, let's look at them in a little more detail.

First, we might say, *"I don't have it."* When you say this, you're often talking about a lack of resources. You don't have the money to send your kid to college. You don't have time or capital to start the side hustle you've always dreamed about.

To your old self, to the version of you that operated out of lack, "I don't have it" would probably have been enough to make you give up and go home. The new you comes from a place of abundance, though. You don't give up just because you don't have enough. You say, "I don't have enough now, but I'll have it when I need it. So I'm going to take the first step. The God who supplies all my needs according to his riches in glory is with me. Christ is in me, so I am enough."

The second excuse we make is, *"I don't know how."* This excuse uses lack of knowledge, skill, or experience to keep you from attempting things that are outside your comfort zone. You don't have the right degree to apply for that job. You've never played that sport before. You aren't good with technology.

> The God who supplies all my needs according to his riches in glory is with me.

But why should ignorance or inexperience get the final word? You've been learning since the day you were born, and you'll keep learning until the day you die. In the age of Google, YouTube, and podcasts, "I don't know how" is more likely to be a cover-up for fear or laziness than a genuine roadblock. The other day I asked a friend of mine if he would ever consider learning to play guitar because he loves guitar so much. He said, "No, at this stage in my life, I'm too old to suck at something." He didn't want to get started because he didn't want to face the moments of failure that go with learning something new.

The old way of doing you might have accepted the "I don't know how" excuse, but the new you looks at failure, mistakes, and starting points differently. The new you is willing to learn along the way, even if that means being embarrassed or changing your mind about some things as you grow. It comes from abundance, choosing to see new paths as opportunities for growth, not failures waiting to happen.

Finally, the third excuse we often fall for is, *"I'm not like them."* This is about comparison. It's driven by a feeling of inadequacy, the infamous imposter syndrome, that causes you to disqualify yourself because you think others are something you are not.

Again, though, that's the old you. The new you knows that the unique way God made you is part of the reason he chose you. The new you says, "My difference *is* my strength. I don't have to hide or change. God is calling me to walk in my strengths, not hide because of my weaknesses. He made me who I am for a reason. He put me here for such a time as this."

> The new you is willing to learn along the way, even if that means being embarrassed or changing your mind about some things as you grow.

Besides, when you say, "I'm not like them," what you mean is, "I'm not like the version of them that I imagine based on the impression I get from them." Most people are just projecting the parts of themselves they want you to see. Don't allow your impression of someone else to become your insecurity about yourself. You don't really know them. I'm sure they have their own share of weaknesses that would cause them to envy your strengths.

Again, Jeremiah's response to God shows all three of these excuses, because Jeremiah was just as human as you and I, and he was painfully aware of what he lacked. It's interesting to me that it wasn't until after Jeremiah listed out his excuses that God gave him what he needed. Jeremiah wrote, *"Then* the LORD reached out his hand and touched my mouth and said to me, 'I have put my words in your mouth'" (verse 9, emphasis added).

You have to feel for Jeremiah. If God's words were already in his mouth, Jeremiah probably wouldn't have said, "Sorry, God, I can't go do that. I can't go speak for you." When he said he didn't know how to speak, that was true—at the moment he said it. But God, who is sovereign, put something in Jeremiah at the moment he needed it.

God is putting something in you too. That's my point. That's what you have to keep at the forefront of your mind and your confession. At this moment, you might not have enough. You might not know enough. You might not be enough. But you'll get it as you go because the God who calls you will also equip and empower you.

Listen to God's reply to Jeremiah. "Do not say, 'I am too young.' You must go to everyone I send you to and say whatever I command you. Do not be afraid of them, for I am with you and will rescue you" (verses 7–8).

Do you hear the echoes of this mindset in God's words to Jeremiah? God was saying, "Jeremiah, people might be against you, but I am with you and I am for you. I am sending you. I am putting my words and my strength within you. I will fight for you, and nobody will be able to withstand you, because I will save you."

God was in it with him, working through him, and fighting for him. That was God's answer to Jeremiah's arguments.

And it's his answer to our arguments too.

When you say, "I'm not," or "I'm only," or "I can't" to a God who is calling you into your future, you're letting something out that's way more valuable than air-conditioning.

You lose the potential God has given you when you speak words that limit you.

When we were first starting our church, I remember a conversation that changed the way I saw myself and spoke about myself. I was riding shotgun beside one of the team members who was helping us start the church. His name was Tyler, and he was our volunteer creative director. We were talking through an idea I had for an upcoming sermon series. Before I shared my idea for the artwork, I threw in a disclaimer. "Now, I know I'm not really creative, but I was wondering if . . ." Then I described my idea.

When I finished he said, "That's a great idea, and I think we should do it. But there's one thing I wish you would never do again."

I waited for him to continue. I thought maybe he was going to say, "I wish you would never tell me how to design sermon artwork. You do the preaching. I'll do the design."

But he didn't. What he said was much more challenging than that. He said, "Don't say, 'I'm not creative.' I've heard you say that more than once. And it actually kind of hurts me when I hear you say it. You're one of the most creative people I've ever met. Just because you don't know how to use Photoshop doesn't mean you're not creative. And I wish you'd stop saying it."

It's weird for me to even think back to that time. Although I still struggle with my inner critic (as you've seen), I *do* accept myself as creative now. I'm made in the image of God. How could I not be creative? I didn't see myself that way back then, but I do now. I'm just glad Tyler had the guts to speak up and say, "Don't say that."

Maybe you need to tell yourself that too. Are you under-mining your potential with the words you let out of your mouth? Are you allowing thoughts that sabotage your confidence and stifle your creativity to wander unchecked through your mind?

If so, be like Tyler. Call yourself out on this. Tell yourself, "Don't say that."

Don't write yourself off with flippant, offhand comments that lock you into the old you. "I'm not good at that. I could never do that. I'm not . . . I can't . . . I won't . . ." If God has called you, he will be with you. And if he is with you, you'll have what you need, when you need it.

Instead of saying, "I don't have it," declare, "God knows what I need before I even ask, and his provision is already on the way."

> Instead of saying, "I don't have it," declare, "God knows what I need before I even ask, and his provision is already on the way."

Instead of saying, "I don't know how," say, "The steps of a good person are guided by the Lord, so he'll lead me as I walk this out."

Instead of saying, "I'm not like them," tell yourself, "I am who I am by the grace of God, and I'm enough for whatever is ahead of me."

Close the doors that are letting in the fear and letting out the confidence. Don't speak things that kill your dreams. Don't downplay your calling. Don't say things that pull you back into the old way of doing you.

Speak life over yourself. Speak grace. Speak hope. Speak what God sees in you and what he says about you.

"I am called, and I am chosen. I might be young, I might be old, I might be inexperienced, I might be overlooked, I might make some mistakes—but I will walk in confidence because God is not against me, but he's in it with me, working through me, fighting for me."

SIXTEEN

GOD IS UP TO SOMETHING UPSTREAM

One of my favorite people to write songs with is my friend Brandon Lake. He lives in Charleston, South Carolina, about three and a half hours away from me.

Recently, we were taking a lunch break during an all-day songwriting session, and he said, "There's something I never told you before. Twelve years ago, when I was eighteen years old, I emailed Elevation Church and asked if I could come learn about songwriting. Somebody wrote back and said, 'No, sorry, we don't have a program like that.' So I kind of gave up on it, but I never forgot about it. And now look where I am."

I didn't know that. It got me thinking. I remembered one time, years ago, I was sitting in my office making chord charts because we didn't have a full-time worship leader. We were a young church, but we were large enough that I was stretched way too thin to be bogged down in technical details. I remember feeling so overwhelmed and asking God who he was going to send to help me.

It was early in our ministry, but I felt like God had put a promise in my heart. I felt that we were going to write and produce worship songs and albums that were going to go around the world, but there I was, hunched over my computer, and it didn't seem like we were anywhere close to touching the world.

I had no idea that at that moment, a few miles away, in Charleston, South Carolina, God was raising up a young man named Brandon, whom I would get to collaborate with in amazing ways. While I was worrying, God was working. While I was praying about something, God was preparing something. I just couldn't see it yet.

I wonder how often the answer to our prayers and our problems is just a few miles away or a few months away. But we can't see what God is doing, so we feel alone. In those moments, we have to engage our faith. We have to choose to walk in confidence knowing that God is in it with us, and he's up to something we can't see.

> We have to choose to walk in confidence knowing that God is in it with us, and he's up to something we can't see.

Earlier we talked about how Israel mourned Moses for a month. Then the period of mourning ended, and it was time to cross the Jordan River and enter the Promised Land. There was a problem, though. The Jordan wasn't a huge river, but it was flood season, so the river was deeper and wider than normal, and the water was flowing quickly. The idea of moving an entire nation across it, including children, livestock, and possessions, would have been overwhelming.

God had a plan, though. He told Joshua to command the priests to carry the ark into the river. Joshua promised everyone that the water would stop flowing so they could cross. But when the priests and the ark started moving toward the river, the water was flowing as fast as ever, and nothing had changed.

Imagine the conversations the people were having as they walked behind the ark. They were stepping forward in faith, but they hadn't seen the miracle yet. They could only follow the ark, which represented God's presence among them. The ark was God "in it with them." It was the promise that God would work through them and fight for them. The whole passage is filled with anticipation about a situation that was very uncertain for the people who were walking into it.

Here's how the Bible describes what happened when the priests reached the river. "Now the Jordan is at flood stage all during harvest. Yet as soon as the priests who carried the ark reached the Jordan and their feet touched the water's edge, the water from upstream stopped flowing. It piled up in a heap a great distance away, at a town called Adam in the vicinity of Zarethan, while the water flowing down to the Sea of the Arabah (that is, the Dead Sea) was completely cut off. So the people crossed over opposite Jericho" (Joshua 3:15–16).

When the priests' feet touched the Jordan, the water stopped flowing. Not when they prayed about the Jordan. Not when they read three books about the Jordan. When they *stepped into the Jordan*. By walking toward uncertainty, they demonstrated their faith for victory. But they didn't see it till they got there. They had to step in faith.

That's where you are going to see the miracle: as you step into it, even though it's awkward and uncomfortable. You must move toward it. You must keep praying, keep believing, keep trusting, keep digging, keep showing up even when it feels fruitless because you know God told you to do it. Your steps may feel uncertain, but God's direction will become clearer as you go.

I realized recently that I've been reading the story about Israel crossing the Jordan a little bit wrong. In my imagination, I pictured it just like the Red Sea: Israel is backed up against the water, the people step into the river, the water stands up into two giant walls, and they walk through. But that's not what the Bible says happened here. It says, "The water from upstream stopped flowing. It piled up in a heap a great distance away" (verse 16).

That means the water stopped flowing upstream so they could cross downstream. It was an *upstream* miracle. It was a miracle hours in the making, and it happened at just the right time. They were wondering how they would cross the river downstream while God was up to something upstream.

This is what I want you to see. You have an upstream God! Your confidence is in a God who knew you'd be in the situation you are in before you got there. He's prepared you for the moment and the moment for you.

> He's prepared you for the moment and the moment for you.

I don't know about you, but I prefer a foolproof, detailed plan before I take a single step. Sometimes Holly will tell me, "Let's go on a walk. It's beautiful outside." The first thing I do is check the weather app. What if it rains while we're walking around the block? Holly will say, "Babe, it's a walk around the block. We're not going to hike the Appalachian Trail. And if we get wet, when we get back, we have towels."

I'm a work in progress. I'm learning to let go of the need to know every obstacle I might face because that's really just a need for control. And my need for control can keep me from going forward. Sometimes it costs me a walk around the block, but sometimes it costs me an opportunity that's much bigger. I have to remind myself that God is in control. I don't need complete knowledge of the weather forecast, and I don't need complete knowledge of the road of life that lies ahead. I need faith to trust him and strength to follow him.

One thing I like to tell myself when I don't feel like I can move forward is, "As I step, God gives me strength." God usually just gives you the next step, and he promises that when you take that step, he'll give you the strength you need. Every step comes with its own strength, and every step makes you stronger.

Say that to yourself. "As I step, God gives me strength." Not, "When I figure it all out" or "When I see the entire road ahead," but when you take the next step of faith. When you get your feet wet in the waters of the Jordan.

What are you stepping toward right now? Maybe it's toward a better version of the parent you wish you would have had, but you didn't, so you're stepping into it even though you don't have a frame of reference for it. As you step, you're getting stronger. As you step, he's making it clearer. As you step, he's making a way.

The story of Israel wading into the water is a picture of step-taking faith, which is real faith. Sometimes I think we need to redefine what we mean by faith in order to really walk in it. Faith can mean almost anything you want it to if you say it in a generic way. When you tell somebody, "I have faith in you," it can just be a nice way of encouraging them.

When you say, "I have faith this is going to work out," it can mean, "I have a good feeling about this."

That's not the kind of faith I need when I'm going through an overflowing Jordan. What I *don't* have when I'm on the bank of a river at flood stage is "a good feeling about this."

I need faith that will help me step through something I *don't* have a good feeling about. I need faith that can take me to the brink of what I know will be a breakthrough even when the floodwaters show no signs of slowing. I need faith to help me step into difficult situations when I don't see how God could possibly work all things together for good.

The good news of the gospel is that this faith doesn't come from us. The faith we have in God was given to us by God. He took the initiative. The Bible says, "For it is by grace you have been saved, through faith—and this is not from yourselves, it is the gift of God" (Ephesians 2:8). Grace is what saves us; faith is what allows us to receive that grace; and both come from above.

Faith isn't something you have to work up. Faith isn't something you have to manufacture. Yes, you have to abide in faith, walk in faith, and grow in faith. But faith is a gift of God, which makes it more about God than about you. It comes from him, it works through you, and it points back to him.

So, if you feel like you have dried-up faith, if you have worn-out faith, if you have broken-down faith, don't condemn yourself. Your faith is not in your faith. It's in the God who sends you faith from another place, who sends you trust from another realm. And since it doesn't come from you, it doesn't depend on you. It comes from God, so it cannot run out. It'll just keep coming with every step and in every situation because God is always up to something upstream.

The town of Adam, where the water started piling up, was about twenty miles up the river. How long does it take water to flow twenty miles? Six hours? I don't know, but God did. Think about the timing of God. The moment their feet got wet, the water dried up. But in order for the water to stop where they were at, it had to have been cut off upstream long before they got there.

God got to Adam six hours earlier than Israel got to the Jordan. He said, "Hey, Jordan River, stop right now because in six hours, the priests' feet are going to hit the water. In six hours, they're going to be on the brink of the promise I made to Abraham four hundred years ago."

Israel had no way of knowing what was happening upstream. Nobody in Adam was texting them saying, "Hey, all the water has been piling up in a heap here, so y'all get ready to cross because the Jordan is going to dry up downstream any minute now."

They couldn't plan it or time it in their own minds. They could only step into it at the instruction of God.

I know it's tempting to wait on God to give you a good feeling before you obey him. We want God to show us on paper how everything's going to work out and then we can trust him. We expect him to take a certain desire away from us and then we will walk in freedom. But the nature of faith is the ability to believe that God is up to something upstream, where we can't see, and the key for us to experience that is to walk toward the thing that stands between us and what God has called us to.

> Faith is the ability to believe that God is up to something upstream.

This could be walking toward freedom, recovery, service, purpose, discipline, restoration, relational intimacy, or a hundred other things. Only you know what God is calling you to walk toward. Maybe you could name one thing God is calling you forward in right now. Maybe you already know the step God is asking you to take.

Ask yourself, "What is something I know God has spoken to me that I can obey today?"

Then do that thing.

When you don't know how to stand or what to do, start doing the thing that you would do if you knew God was in it with you, working through you, fighting for you. Do the thing you would do if you believed he's been working upstream all along.

"But I'm not certain how it's going to turn out." Well, do the thing that you would do if you were certain that God was with you.

"Are you saying I could just start anything and assume that God is with me? Are you saying I can open a coffee shop and the Lord is going to bless it?" I don't know. You might not know how to run a business, and I've never tasted your coffee, so that's between you, God, and people who can give you some honest feedback. But if you are following his presence and he's calling you to step into a promise he gave you, then do the thing that you would do if you knew that twenty miles upstream, he was already at work.

You don't know what God is up to upstream. That's why you can't die downstream. That's why you have to step into the Jordan. That's why you have to do the thing that you would do if you believed victory, healing, breakthrough, second chances, and new beginnings were on the other side.

Remember, wherever you have a problem, heaven has a plan. Turn the outcome over to the Lord and leave it there.

Then, take the step.

Will you trust him with the twenty miles in between? Will you try your best not to stress for these next two weeks while you wait for the test results? While you wait for the MRI appointment, will you put it in his hands?

You're going to have some downstream doubts. Me, you, the pope, the bishop, the attorney general, and your praying grandmother all have doubts downstream. When you can't see God doing it, when you can't feel God doing it, you'll start to wonder sometimes if you're crazy for trusting God.

Doubts don't indicate lack of faith, though, because doubts are mostly feelings, and faith is mostly action. You are more than your doubts. They are leftover habits from the old you, but that's not you anymore. Do the thing *the new you* would do: the you God is speaking to. The you God is flowing through. The you that is in harmony with him. The you that is sustained by grace. The you that is full of the faith of Jesus Christ. Let God deal with the things you can't deal with as you do the things he has called you to do.

> Let God deal with the things you can't deal with as you do the things he has called you to do.

Maybe you are on the brink of a breakthrough. You're standing on the bank of the river, about to dip your big toe into it. Maybe you're going to call a counselor this week and say, "I'm ready to start working on my issues." Maybe you're going to reach out to someone with an apology. Maybe you're going to buy a canvas and paints because something inside you is telling you to take up art again. Maybe you'll invite someone over for dinner because you're tired of being lonely. Those are steps, and that is faith.

While you're taking baby steps into rushing rivers, God is up to mighty miracles twenty miles away. He's up to something in the unseen. He's up to something in the unexpected. He's up to something in the hidden place. He's up to something in the shadows. You can count on that.

It might not happen in the next twenty minutes. It might not happen in the next twenty days. The timeframe is God's business. But if you can believe him, if you can take the steps the new you would take and do the things the new you would do, you're going to see the miracle.

What is starting at this moment didn't start at this moment because God was twenty miles ahead of you. And God will give you strength to match every one of your steps. Don't turn back now!

You can't control the river, but you can walk toward it. You can step into it. And when you do, you'll see the fulfillment of what God has already set in motion.

SEVENTEEN

MAKE PEACE WITH YOUR STRENGTH

Growing up in the South, I often heard people use this phrase: "You're getting too big for your britches." It meant you had started to think too highly of yourself.

In church and later on in seminary, a religious version of that was instilled in me. It usually went along with Proverbs 16:18. "Pride goes before destruction, a haughty spirit before a fall." I understood early on if you did something good, you had to give God all the credit; and if you did something bad, you had to take all the blame. I'm not saying this was taught directly, but you kind of just picked it up. You could talk about your failures all you wanted because that was humility. But you had to be careful when you talked about what you had accomplished because you might be getting caught up in pride, and that was the sin that got the devil kicked out of heaven.

To this day I often find myself dealing with a subconscious fear when I celebrate the good things that are happening because I worry I might be getting too big for my britches.

I wonder if God is going to humble me somehow just to put me in my place.

Now, it's definitely a bad idea to think you accomplished something in your own strength that God enabled you to do, or to allow an accomplishment to make you think you're better than someone else, or to assume you're above tripping and falling around the next corner. I get that, and I'm sure you do too.

But the belief that I shouldn't feel good about something I've done is kind of messed up, isn't it? What if my kids viewed me the same way I've often viewed God? "Be careful what you say around Dad. If he thinks you're proud of what you've accomplished, if he sees you taking credit for your good grades or your wrestling trophy or a picture you drew, he'll take you down a notch. He'll humble you just to teach you a lesson."

Can you see how toxic that belief is? That's why the first part of this affirmation—"God is not against me"—is foundational to the rest of it. If we are going to walk in faith, if we are going to be and do all the things God has put inside us, we can't start from a place of "God is out to get me." That's a path that leads to paralysis, not possibility.

I know I owe everything to God's grace. I've worked hard and done my best, but I could never do enough to deserve all the blessings I have. I could never do enough to earn all the opportunities God has given me. I don't for a moment think I can work my way into heaven. I know full well that pride is a sneaky, subtle enemy and staying humble is my responsibility.

But God has been teaching me to think differently about the strengths he's given me. He's teaching me to make peace not just with my weaknesses, not just with my past, not just with my failures and limitations—but with my *strengths*. With my gifts. With my calling.

I believe he's asking the same thing of you. I believe he gets excited when you do great things. I think it makes him proud.

My son Elijah has released two albums now. They aren't platinum-selling albums, of course—he's just getting started, and he's just going to get better and better as he makes music throughout his life. But the fact that a seventeen-year-old has already put two albums into the world with songs he wrote and recorded himself is something worth celebrating. As I watched him conceptualize album art, push through his insecurities to shoot music videos, and find his own confidence as he combined the music that he loves with his life experience, I never felt the need to "bring him down a notch." I didn't try to make sure he gave me enough credit for buying his recording equipment or for encouraging him through the process. He's my son, and he's stepping into his calling and gifting and dreams, and that makes me happy. I know parts of that journey will be awkward, and I know he's a work in progress, but as his father, I celebrated every step.

How much more excited do you think God gets when you use the strengths he gave you? He's happy to see you step into the potential he put inside you. Can you imagine God feeling proud of you? Can you imagine God praising you? Can you imagine God promoting you?

Because that's what he does. That's who he is. That's how he thinks. That's how he sees you.

When Proverbs says that pride goes before destruction, it doesn't mean God wants you to call yourself a worm and grovel in the dirt. It just means you shouldn't put all your trust in your own ability. It means you don't claim you are the sole source of all the good things you've received. It means that while you walk in your *strength*, you keep trusting in your *God*. Those things are not mutually exclusive. They work together.

That's what I mean by making peace with your strength. It's not pride to see your strengths. It's a perspective of faith. And it pleases God because he's the one who put those things in you in the first place.

> While you walk in your *strength*, you keep trusting in your *God*. Those things are not mutually exclusive. They work together.

Are you an artist? Are you good at math? Are you a people person? Are you a natural at business? Do you like public speaking? Are you athletic? Do you love solving problems? Are you a gifted motivator? Those are not minor details. Those are not accidental qualities. God put strength in you. He knows it, and hopefully you know it too. You need to be willing to walk in it without thinking God is going to smite you from heaven if you dare to dream big.

It's become very popular in recent years to share your vulnerabilities and accept them openly in order to connect with others and be okay with the way you are. There's a place for all of that, and we've discussed it quite a bit in this book. But self-acceptance should also include accepting your strengths. Don't just say, "Look at all the things I can't do. I'm just going to sit around and watch other people do stuff on YouTube for hours rather than trying to do anything myself." No, you have to notice your gifts. You have to value your experience. You have to pay attention to your point of view and the doors God has set before you.

I think sometimes we don't make peace with our strengths because we know that if we do, we're responsible to use them. But then, what if we fail? It's easier to say that the time isn't right, that we need more experience, that someone else is better suited for the job.

As we saw earlier, that's exactly what Gideon tried to do when God first called him. I want to look at his story again because Gideon was really good at accepting his weaknesses, but he had a harder time accepting his strengths. He struggled to look past his small, depressed view of himself and to accept that he was meant for much more.

Remember, at the beginning of the story, the angel and Gideon had a sort of passive-aggressive argument. The angel said Gideon was a mighty warrior, and Gideon ignored that and said God had abandoned them. So the angel ignored *that* and said, "Go in the strength you have and save Israel out of Midian's hand. Am I not sending you?" Finally Gideon replied, "But how can I save Israel? My clan is the weakest in Manasseh, and I am the least in my family" (Judges 6:14–15).

Do you see how hard Gideon was fighting *not* to believe in himself? How fiercely and faithfully he defended a low view of his potential because that seemed safer than recognizing the gifts and callings God had placed within him? He was flat-out refusing to acknowledge the power strength within him and the grace upon him.

God wasn't about to lose the argument, though. He finally convinced Gideon to see himself as God saw him and to believe that God was with him, and that set him on a course to become one of the greatest deliverers in Israel's history.

What about you? Are you engaged in an argument with a God who sees the strengths he gave you and won't stop until you see them too? If so, will you let him win? Will you agree to go in your strength into the victory God is giving you? Or will you shrink down to the level of your past, to your fear, to your feelings, to the stuff you left behind, to the insecurity that keeps you stuck inside yourself?

God knows you, and you know you. But maybe you don't know the same you. See, like Gideon, you can be weak and strong at the same time. The strength and weakness that live inside of you are meant to coexist. One doesn't cancel out the other. That's why you have to accept both your weaknesses and your strengths.

The weakness teaches you to depend on Jesus. If you didn't have any weakness, you would think you didn't need Jesus, and you probably *would* get too big for your britches. The strength exists to show you what God and you can do together. It gives you confidence to say, "I can do all things through Christ who strengthens me." It gives you faith in a God who is able to do immeasurably more than you ask or think according to his power that works in you. A God who fills you up, who makes you able to climb a mountain, who makes you able to live again, who makes you able to break out of those chains.

The defining moment in the argument came when Gideon offered the angel something to eat. The angel touched the food with his staff, and fire instantly consumed the meal. Gideon realized this wasn't just an angel he was talking to. This was God. Immediately he assumed he was going to die because he had seen God face-to-face.

Can I tell you something? When God shows us who he really is and tells us what we can do through his presence and power, the first thing we often feel is fear. I know fear gets a bad rap, but every feeling of fear we get isn't an indication that something is wrong. Sometimes it's God breaking through our senses and our limited experience and showing up in our situation. So if you find fear rise up when you face something challenging, don't duck back into the winepress. Don't hide in who you used to be. God is calling you into the new you, and that will take a little getting used to.

God told Gideon, "Peace! Do not be afraid. You are not going to die" (verse 23). Then Gideon built an altar on the spot and called it "The Lord Is Peace."

Think about that for a moment. God showed up, the food burned up, Gideon got all worked up—and then he realized this was *friendly* fire. God wasn't there to judge him but to anoint him. Like Moses at the burning bush, like the tongues of fire at Pentecost, this was God showing up in his all-consuming love and power and goodness to call Gideon into his true self.

The God of Peace is the one who calls you to go in strength. In other words, making peace with your strength starts by knowing God is at peace with you. He's not against you; he's for you. The peace you have *with* God and *in* God is what gives you confidence to carry out his purpose.

When you make peace with your strength, you recognize that since the strength comes from God, it depends on God. You say, "These are the gifts you've given me. These are the abilities you've entrusted to me. Sometimes I don't feel like much, but you're calling me mighty, and you're saying I have strengths, so I'm going to go in whatever I've got."

Maybe you find yourself thinking, *I could be a more patient person. I could be more encouraging. I could apply for that job.* Maybe you could! Go in the strength you have and find out. Don't disqualify yourself by quitting before you even have a chance to succeed. Don't hide in a winepress and call it humility if God is telling you to move forward in faith.

That night, God told Gideon to tear down an altar that his father had built to Baal, a false god, then to build a new altar and sacrifice one of his father's bulls to the true God. So Gideon did it. You've got to give him credit for that. He had moments of fear, but he also did some pretty courageous things.

> When you make peace with your strength, you recognize that since the strength comes from God, it depends on God.

The next day, all the neighbors were angry and wanted to kill Gideon, but Gideon's father said, "Hey, if Baal is really a god, let him defend himself." Of course, Baal didn't, and Baal couldn't, because God was with Gideon, and God is with you.

There's a lesson here. I think a lot of us never make peace with the strength we have, the capacity we have, the potential we have, because we are limited by what we've always seen and known. Often, the first step to making peace with who God made you to be is to smash some altars from the past.

I don't mean that literally. I'm not saying you should go through your dad's garage and throw out his power tools because he spent too much time out there and not enough with you. I don't mean if your parents drank too much, you should run through the house breaking all their liquor bottles. That should be obvious.

I mean it metaphorically. Make a break with the things from the past that told you who you were and who you weren't. Gideon had to stop saying he was the littlest member of the weakest family in the smallest tribe. He had to reject the false beliefs of his family and neighbors and embrace what God was showing him.

There may be some altars you need to smash, some beliefs you need to renounce, some assumptions you need to question. "Everybody in our family has a drinking problem. Nobody in our family went to college. Everybody I know has blown up their marriage. None of my coworkers have a good work ethic."

For Gideon to build an altar called "The Lord Is Peace" and to go in the strength he had meant leaving behind the life he was used to and loyal to. It meant moving on from the people he had always known, the patterns he had always followed, and the perspective he had chosen for himself.

Breaking out of the past is not easy. Making peace with your strength isn't easy. Sometimes you minimize what God is doing so you can fit it into your previous experience. God is calling you up higher, but if he is saying something about you that you've never seen in you, it might scare you. "I can't do that. That's not me."

But what if it *is* you? What if the other stuff—the fear, the holding back, the negativity, the going through life guarded, the avoiding responsibility, the not being creative, the not wanting to lead, the lack of discipline, the lack of follow-through—is the false stuff? What if "wimp in a winepress" is just where fear has put you, but "mighty warrior" is who God calls you?

If you read the rest of the story, God did an incredible miracle through Gideon and three hundred soldiers armed with nothing but torches, trumpets, and jars. They didn't have a massive army, and they didn't even have conventional weapons, but they had faith. Faith in a God who was for them, not against them. Faith in a God who worked through them and fought on their side.

God calls you a mighty warrior, but you're looking around for a mighty army. Maybe there isn't one. The might isn't in the size of the army, it's in the size of the God in you. It's Christ in you. That has always been enough, and it will always make you enough.

Make peace with your strength because the God of Peace gave it to you. Don't fight the fire God has given you. Don't fight the flow he has given you. Don't downplay yourself to placate people who aren't going where God is taking you. Don't fight what you're good at to fit in with what you weren't meant for to begin with. Don't worship at the altar of everything your family knew.

Yes, you'll feel fear at times. But the answer to your fear isn't to shrink what God speaks to fit the context of what you've known. The answer isn't to hide out and hope someone else answers the call.

The answer is to expand into everything God says you are. Accept your Self, the one he created you to be, and rely on him.

Do the thing *that* you would do. The mighty warrior you. The capable you. The called you. The confident you. The you that has made peace with your strength.

What you tell yourself matters, which is why it's so important to remind yourself that God is not against you, but he's in it with you, working through you, fighting for you. The more you can believe that affirmation, the more confidence you'll have as you step into your future.

One of the greatest challenges we face as we take these steps of faith is to guard our hearts and minds from negativity. I'm not talking about ignoring reality. I'm talking about making sure we don't interpret life through the wrong filters: things like doubt, fear, insecurity, negativity, and hopelessness.

We have to take what we know to be true about God and live it out on the level of our feelings and actions. We have to choose the *right* filter for our life experiences, which brings us to our next mindset. It's the shortest but maybe the most practical of them all: *My joy is my job.*

MINDSET (05)

MY JOY IS MY JOB.

ACTION STEP:
OWN YOUR EMOTIONS.

EIGHTEEN

THE HARD WORK OF HAPPINESS

A couple years ago, while we were on vacation having lunch, I asked my family, "Who's the happiest person you know?" I'm famous for starting games like this at family meals, and my kids are famous for finding the inherent flaws in them.

They said, "That's kind of an impossible question. You can't really know if people are happy or not."

They had a point. But I kept pushing, so they started listing the happiest people they knew. I was surprised by some of their answers, but I was not surprised that none of them said, "You, Dad."

Don't get me wrong. I can be a pretty fun guy. But I wasn't expecting to get the Happiest Human Alive Award, or even the Happiest Dad Award, for that matter. Still, part of me was hoping at least one of them would give me an honorable mention. I was paying for their vacation. I had even ordered appetizers. So before it was Holly's turn, I teed it up for her. I said, "Holly, *you* are the happiest person I know."

It wasn't flattery: it was true. She replied, "That's so sweet." And then she said somebody else's name as her answer.

The conversation gave me a lot to think about. I've been told more than once that I have a tendency to look . . . serious, shall I say. Or mad. Or even mean. Some people's natural expression is "resting blessed face." I have the other kind of RBF, apparently.

And, if I'm really honest, I'm *not* an automatically optimistic person. My first instinct in a situation is to see vulnerabilities, liabilities, and obstacles. If I can't find any, I'll keep looking. I am a creative locator of things to fear and dread. That's the guy whom Holly, the happiest person I know, gets to live with.

Brian Wilson from the Beach Boys once said, "I'm 70 years old and it took me a long time to learn a really simple thing: it's hard work to be happy."* I get that. I've seen that. I've found that it's not easy to own my emotions. It's hard work to manage my feelings. I have to lean into this liberating little phrase: *My joy is my job.* I say that to myself a lot, and it's a good reminder to keep my feelings and attitude in check.

The psalmist wrote, "This is the day the LORD has made; We will rejoice and be glad in it" (Psalm 118:24 NKJV). *Will rejoice* means joy is an act of the will. It's within our control. There is great hope in that because it means we get to choose the energy and enthusiasm we carry into our day.

---

* Random House of Canada Limited, news release (April 15, 2013), "Rock & roll music legend Brian Wilson to publish new memoir with Random House Canada," https://www.newswire.ca/news-releases/rock--roll-music -legend-brian-wilson-to-publish-new-memoir-with-random-house-canada -512265701.html.

I like calling it the "hard work of happiness" because you have to work hard at it sometimes. Some of us more than others, apparently. But doesn't working on happiness sound like a contradiction? Work isn't usually associated with fun. Work is what you push through so you can make it to the weekend and *have* fun. Happiness should be easy, shouldn't it? We should wake up in the morning with a bounce in our step and go through our day with positive vibes only. Or so we've been told, and so we tell ourselves, even though it doesn't work that way.

The reality is that your emotions and thoughts move all over the place. They shift and change without warning. You can wake up excited and full of hope, then see one text from the night before and lose your joy by 7:45 in the morning. Or you can be in a funk driving home in the evening, but a song you love comes on as you're turning into the driveway, and the negativity you carried the whole day evaporates in two seconds.

Your feelings matter, but feelings can be fickle. Both of those things are true.

That's where the work comes in.

You have to manage your emotions. You have to frame your feelings within the larger context of who you are. You are an emotional person, but you are not your emotions.

Now, I didn't say bury your feelings. I didn't say hate them, hide them, or feel guilty for them. I didn't say just move on after that breakup broke your heart and pretend you're fine if you're not. I didn't say to keep all the stress you're under bottled up inside until you hit a wall and start having panic attacks.

I said *own your emotions*. Take authority over your attitudes. Acknowledge the things that are rushing through your head and heart and respond to them appropriately. Intentionally. Maturely.

Like the new you would do.

> Joy, satisfaction, contentment, gratitude, forgiveness, freedom, and confidence are all growing within you because of the presence and power of the Holy Spirit.

The old you thought happiness came from the outside. It was something you chased, earned, built, or demanded.

The new you knows that happiness comes from *within* you. Peace is inside you because the God of Peace is always with you. Joy, satisfaction, contentment, gratitude, forgiveness, freedom, and confidence are all growing within you because of the presence and power of the Holy Spirit. That's what the fruit of the Spirit is, after all. It's what God does in you, not just what circumstances produce for you.

Owning your emotions means that *you* are central to the process. Your joy is your job. Your attitude is your assignment. Your stability is your responsibility. It's nobody else's job to make you happy. Your spouse doesn't have that obligation. Or your kids. Or your boss. Or your dog. They can be there for you, but they can't shoulder the weight of your happiness. They would suffocate under that kind of expectation because your joy isn't within their jurisdiction. Only you can answer for your attitude.

One time I made the mistake of saying somebody stole my joy, and the Holy Spirit really called me out on it. "They stole your joy? Your joy is not their job, and if they stole it you should have done a better job locking the doors so they couldn't get to it. If someone else can steal your joy, that means you're keeping your joy where anybody can come along and snatch it."

I might not be the happiest guy my family knows, but that doesn't mean I have to be the grumpiest one. My joy is my job, and I'm determined to be up for the task. Traffic jams can't steal my joy. The stressful meeting at work can't steal my tranquility. Those aches and pains that started when I turned forty can't steal my contentment, because all these things are mine to manage.

As I said, I had to learn how this works. I remember a few years ago we were launching a new sermon series in our church, and we had record attendance. Every overflow room in the church was packed to maximum capacity. Across so many of our campuses, I was hearing reports about how high the attendance numbers were.

And yet, between services, I found myself sitting backstage, feeling dead inside. In fact, I couldn't feel anything. I had preached with all my heart, and I was grateful for what God was doing. But if I'm honest, so much of my happiness had hung on the goal of having a huge Sunday that when we surpassed that goal, it felt a little empty. It was one of the biggest moments of our ministry, and for reasons I'm still coming to understand, I felt like crying, not celebrating.

I pushed myself back out there and preached again, but I was pretty shaken up by what I had felt. I thought, *If I don't feel happy now, when will I?* I told myself, *I probably need a break. I'm exhausted. I just need to get away.*

A short while later, we did get away. Holly and I were invited to spend a week on one of the most beautiful islands I've ever seen. The person who invited us insisted on covering all the expenses, so we didn't even have any financial pressure hanging over our heads. But for some reason, I was sad the entire time. I actually felt as if I were in prison on that island. My wife was there, my friends were there, but I wasn't there. Well, I was there—but I wasn't there. And the absence of joy in the presence of so much goodness really scared me.

On the way home, I told Holly, "I think I need to get some help. I don't think I'm in a good place."

She didn't rub it in my face. She didn't say, "I told you so," even though she had told me several times that she thought I might need to consider meeting with a counselor to process all the pressure I was under.

I always resisted that for the same reasons we often resist getting help. I thought if I just pushed through, tried harder, hit more goals, and improved my environment, my feelings and thoughts and insecurities would take care of themselves. I was on that treadmill of chasing, and never quite catching up with "Future You" I talked about earlier. The problem was within me though, not around me. I saw that clearly on the island.

My mindset up until that point was that if I could just reach a certain goal or experience a greater level of success, then I would be enough. I would be worthy, and I would be happy. But I was burying some stuff I needed to deal with and carrying some stuff I needed to set down, and it was burning me out.

Now, it's not that my life was a disaster or everything was falling apart. I'm not saying every day was a dark, gloomy pit of despair. I experienced amazing moments while carrying all of these burdens. But I knew that in order to be the man I wanted my kids to see—and hopefully someone they would want to imitate a little bit—there was some work I needed to do. Not work on the church, but work on *myself*. And not just to have moments of worldly happiness either, but to have God's joy as the reference point for my soul.

The old mindset was killing me and the new me was calling me, but it wouldn't come easy. First, I had to find someone to talk to. That required admitting to another human being that I needed help. For someone who likes to be thought of as the strong one, that was hard to do. But I did it. I reached out to a friend and asked, "Who's that therapist you met with years ago? Would you make an introduction for me?"

My friend was glad to help. It turns out that although your joy is your job, when you really commit to it, you'll usually find allies who will assist you in the battle.

That began a process of weekly therapy that I've been committed to for over five years now. I won't spend too much time talking about it here because so many of the lessons that I've already shared have been the fruit of that life-altering process.

According to my wife, other people who know me well, and the inward witness of the Holy Spirit, I'm in a much better place now. Not only because of therapy, but because of a commitment to the deep, analytical work of putting off old ways of doing me and putting on new ones.

Learning about ourselves is not contrary to following Christ. It is the *consequence* of following Christ. God is a God of truth, and truth sets us free. God uses many messengers to deliver his truth. He used a donkey to show Balaam his blind spots, and he can certainly use trained professionals to show us ours.

My point isn't that you need therapy. Maybe you do, maybe you don't. Maybe you tried it and it didn't work. Or maybe you tried it but *you* didn't do the work. I don't know. I've learned that for some people, therapy is a tool; for others, it becomes a weapon. After processing all their problems, they come to the conclusion that talking about it isn't helping, and they feel even worse.

Regardless of the tools you use, you have to own your emotions. You have to understand some things about yourself, about your upbringing, about your mental models, about your personality, about trauma from the past. That is part of the hard work of happiness because you are reclaiming the narrative of you, of the new you, and that's a good thing. That's a godly thing.

Emotions are valuable, of course. You have to pay attention to how you feel. How else would you know when to rest? How else would you know what God is leading you to do if there were no sensation of prompting from the Holy Spirit? There are some things you have to feel out, not just reason out, so feelings and emotions and desires have a place.

> Learning about ourselves is not contrary to following Christ. It is the *consequence* of following Christ. God is a God of truth, and truth sets us free.

But that place is not the throne of our lives.

God is on the throne. That means what God speaks, what he wants, the bigger picture of where he's taking your life and how he wants to use you—that should carry the greatest weight, even when you aren't really "feeling it."

We tend to put our feelings on the throne. If we want to go off about something, we go off. If we want to sleep in, we sleep in. If we want to skip leg day, we skip leg day. If we feel like doing something sinful to feel relief in a stressful moment, we justify it: "Oh, it's not that bad." We let our feelings tell us what is best, what is true, what is right.

But feelings aren't meant to be followed. They're meant to be conditioned and conformed to the image of Christ.

The passage we've been looking at in Ephesians 4 says that the old self "is being corrupted by its deceitful desires" (verse 22). The problem with *deceitful* desires is that, by definition, you don't know they are wrong. You can have cravings, feelings, emotions, and needs that present themselves to you as absolute truth, but they aren't what they claim to be. They are sneaky. They are subtle. They are convincing. But they are not always right.

> But feelings aren't meant to be followed. They're meant to be conditioned and conformed to the image of Christ.

Many times in my life, I've been pummeled and punished by the consequences of things I thought I wanted. I bet you have too. The anger that felt so right in the moment. The lie that was so helpful in getting what you wanted. The critical conversation about someone else that made you feel better about yourself, but only for a few seconds. The slammed door that got your point across to your spouse.

But at what cost?

The new you is called to see through those unchecked urges. It's the version of you that sees deceitful desires for what they are: flashbacks to the old you.

How do you identify which desires are deceitful? How do you walk in the new you instead of reverting to the old you?

Let me give you three simple steps. Think of the word *NEW* as an acronym.

Notice
Evaluate
Walk In

That last one isn't quite as smooth as the first two, but it's the most important.

Notice means you have to pay attention to your thoughts, your reactions, your feelings, your fears, your desires. In case you never go to therapy, I want to make sure you get this basic psychology foundation: you can't deal with things you don't know are there. You can't make good choices when you don't even realize you're choosing.

So pay attention to your fear. Listen to your anger. Take note when something within you gets triggered. "There I am, blaming people again. There I am, catastrophizing again." Notice it, but then remind yourself that you're not it.

Next, *evaluate* the thing you've noticed. Is this desire good or bad? Is this action right or wrong? Is this decision wise or unwise? Don't just shrug your shoulders and say, "That's just me. That's how I've always been. That's how my dad was too. Oh well." Compare that thing to what God says about you. Evaluate whether it's the new you or the old you.

When fear comes, I try to frame it this way in my mind: "I'm feeling fear." This gives me some distance so I can deal with the fear for what it is. This is more than just semantics. If I say, "I *am* afraid," that pushes me toward an identity. I don't want to be scared Steven. Scared Steven does dumb things. He lashes out, he snaps at people, he makes shortsighted decisions. On the other hand, if I say, "I'm *feeling* fear," then I'm simply acknowledging a fact. The emotion is valid, but it's not going to last forever. It's like stormy weather: it will pass. It's not who I am. Jesus is in me, and Jesus isn't scared, so scared Steven isn't the real me.

I *notice* the fear like I would check the weather. I *evaluate* it. Then I *walk in* the me that I'm meant to be, carrying an umbrella if I have to. I choose to walk in faith and courage because that's the true me.

I'm not back in the eighties here, flippantly singing, "Don't worry, be happy." I'm just reminding you that in Christ, your joy is not held hostage by anything or anyone. It's yours. Jesus gave it to you. The world didn't. And as the old gospel song says, "If the world didn't give it, the world can't take it away."*

Jesus told his disciples, "Peace I leave with you; my peace I give you. I do not give to you as the world gives. Do not let your hearts be troubled and do not be afraid" (John 14:27). Later he said to them, "You will grieve, but your grief will turn to joy . . . I will see you again and you will rejoice, and no one will take away your joy" (John 16:20, 22).

God gives you a peace that the world can't give you. He gives you a joy nobody can steal from you. Even when the world is shifting and quaking around you, his peace is your peace. His joy is your joy. His confidence is your confidence.

You don't have to be the most cheerful, extroverted, life-of-the-party person on the outside. That's okay. Your family

---

* Written and performed by Shirley Caesar, "The World Didn't Give It to Me" (HOB, 1975).

loves you anyway. Besides, your seriousness might be part of what paid for the vacation.

On the inside, though, you can know that your joy is real, and it's yours, and you're growing more and more each day into the image of Christ in you.

NINETEEN

WHO'S IN YOUR HEAD?

Joey Logano is a NASCAR driver and two-time Cup Series champion. He's a friend of our family and part of our church, and I'm a big fan. Of Joey, that is, not NASCAR. I don't really understand the intricacies of the sport, but I love Joey.

The first time I took my family to a race, it was because Joey talked me into it. I was a little hesitant. I said, "I totally respect what you do, but wouldn't it be kind of boring to watch you drive around in circles for four hours?"

He said, "Trust me, bring the kids. They'll love it."

We met his crew at the Charlotte Motor Speedway, and they gave us VIP treatment. We each got a little radio and a yellow headset so we could hear the crew chief and the spotter telling Joey what to do. Listening to the inside communication was a lot of fun.

Abbey was five years old at the time. She was obsessed with that yellow headset, but she was a little confused about how it worked. She thought Joey could hear her too. So she started talking to him. "Joey Wogano. Joey Wogano. Can you hear me, Joey Wogano?"

We were all having so much fun watching her that none of us had the heart to tell her, "Baby, he can't hear you." Joey was driving around the track at 185 miles per hour, and a five-year-old thought she was giving him instructions. Of course he couldn't hear her. He has a crew chief and a spotter who talk to him while he's driving, and that's about it. Everyone else can yell and shout and cuss and cheer from a distance, but they don't get a direct line to his ear.

But what if they did? Imagine if Joey's team stood at the gate and told every fan, "Here's your radio and headset so you can say whatever you want to Joey. Any advice, any corrections, any trash talk. Have at it."

What if he could hear all those voices in his headset in real time? Uncle Bubba would be up there weighing in on what Joey should do: "Turn left. Turn left again!" That's about all Uncle Bubba knows about racing. The fastest car he ever had was a Maxima. Do you think Uncle Bubba should get to tell Joey how to drive?

It would ruin Joey's focus. It would wreck his concentration. Nobody could race right with all those voices in their head.

And nobody can *live* right with all those voices in their head either. Nobody can navigate the challenges of life with steadiness and courage if they make every critic and commentator a copilot.

And yet, isn't that what a lot of us do? We give everybody a mic. "Here you go, CNN. Here you go, Fox News. Here you go, Elon. Here you go, TikTok. Here you go, random internet troll with seventeen followers and a chip on your shoulder." To be honest, often the loudest voice of all is the old self, the old you, that still tries to control your course.

I'm not saying it's wrong to listen to other voices if they're actually helpful, but they aren't your crew chief. They aren't your spotter. You can't afford to let every voice have the same access to your attention and your emotions.

> If you're going to manage your joy, you have to manage your focus.

Here's my point. If you're going to manage your joy, you have to manage your focus.

Earlier we talked about how Joshua had to lead Israel across the Jordan at flood stage. Before God did an upstream miracle for Israel, he had a heart-to-heart conversation with Joshua about focus.

Remember, Moses was gone now, and Joshua had recently been put in charge. That could not have been the most peaceful transition in Joshua's life. Not only was he taking over command from the only leader the nation had ever known, which meant every move he made would be scrutinized and compared to how Moses would have done it, but he also had to lead the people into situations that didn't make any sense and into battles that were bigger than anything they had faced before.

I'm sure every general, every commander, every soldier, and every citizen had an opinion about what they should do next. Joshua couldn't have all those voices in his head. So God gave him some advice about whom he needed to listen to and what he needed to focus on.

> Be strong and very courageous. Be careful to obey all
> the law my servant Moses gave you; do not turn from
> it to the right or to the left, that you may be successful
> wherever you go. Keep this Book of the Law always
> on your lips; meditate on it day and night, so that you
> may be careful to do everything written in it. Then
> you will be prosperous and successful. Have I not
> commanded you? Be strong and courageous. Do not
> be afraid; do not be discouraged, for the LORD your
> God will be with you wherever you go. (Joshua
> 1:7–9)

Notice two things here. First, God told Joshua to obey the law, keep it on his lips, and meditate on it. That means his actions, words, and thoughts needed to be aligned with faith. For faith to be effective, it must be *focused*. Second, God told Joshua several times not to be afraid or discouraged but to be strong and *courageous*.

I think God was telling Joshua that his focus and his courage were connected. He knew Joshua was going to face a lot of risky, scary situations. He knew fear and discouragement were always going to be a temptation. He wanted Joshua to know that in the moments when negative emotions were trying to shut him down and a thousand voices were telling him what he was doing wrong and why he was going to fail, he would need to focus his faith.

We need to do the same thing. We need to learn to overcome fear and discouragement by meditating on what God says, speaking what God says, and doing what God says.

Most of us don't naturally do this. We don't focus our faith on God; we focus our fear on the problem in front of us. "I'm discouraged because I haven't gotten a promotion in five years. I'm discouraged because I can't pay off my school loan. I'm discouraged because my back pain is getting worse, not better."

Instead of dealing with what's inside of us, we complain about what's in front of us. "Oh, being married is my problem. If I were only single . . ." Are you sure that would help? Because three years ago, you said, "Oh, if I were only married . . ." Which one is it?

I'm not saying your problems are in your head. They are real, and they are challenging, and it's normal to feel fear and frustration. But are you making them worse by listening to the wrong voices? Are you letting fear be your crew chief? Have you made frustration your spotter? Maybe the discouragement you're feeling is coming less from what you're facing and more from what you're telling yourself *about* what you are facing.

The Bible says that faith comes by hearing the word of God. The opposite is also true: discouragement comes by hearing the words of the world, the whispers of worry, the arguments of anxiety. If you are dealing with fear and discouragement, go back and take a look at your dialogue. Not the dialogue you're having with others, although that can be part of it, but the dialogue you have on the inside. Notice if you're listening to the voice of fear, the voice of doubt, the voice of the old you.

God was saying, "Joshua, in order to be strong, in order to stay encouraged, you need to narrow your focus. Don't just do whatever comes into your head or whatever people tell you to do. Obey the Word, speak the Word, meditate on the Word. Focus your faith on the path I laid out for you, and you'll be successful."

Again, you're going to feel some anxious things, and that's okay. God wasn't trying to stop Joshua from *feeling* fear or discouragement. God wasn't saying, "Stop being so dramatic. Stop being so emotional. Stop crying or I'll give you something to cry about."

He didn't say, "Don't *feel* discouraged."

He said, "Don't *be* discouraged."

There is a big difference to God between what you feel and who you are. Your condition is not your identity. Maybe you're feeling worried right now, but that's how you feel, not who you are. Maybe you're afraid right now, but that's your condition, not your identity.

God is not talking about a feeling here at all.

He's talking about a focus.

He's saying, "That's fine you feel it, but don't *be* it. That's okay you feel it, but don't *behave* like it."

You don't have to believe everything fear tells you. You don't have to accept every negative thought that pops into your head. They might not be true at all. They might not be the whole story. They might not be the right perspective. You need a security checkpoint in your brain, one of those TSA agents with no sense of humor at the entrance of your mind telling certain thoughts, "You're not coming past this point."

If you are in a conversation with yourself all the time that doesn't involve God and you're not letting him interrupt your thoughts, chances are, you're going to get discouraged. Not because circumstances themselves are so hard—although they might be—but because self-talk can be brutal. If you're not managing your meditation, the enemy will try to sneak in and steal your hope. "Man, that situation is impossible. There's no way out of that." Or he's going to get you with worry. When your kids drive off to go to school, he'll say, "They're going to crash. They're going to die in a car wreck."

I'm not trying to make you into some machine or say that you can always control what thoughts come in your mind, but you have more control than the enemy wants you to believe. You have to *choose* to focus, though. You have to be intentional about this or you'll default to the old you.

If you're careful what you let in you, you'll be courageous when you face what's ahead. Be open to voices that help you, but don't elevate anyone to the level of God's Word. The Holy Spirit is your crew chief and your spotter. Listen to his voice. Meditate on it and obey it. Speak what he says to yourself, not what fear, discouragement, or Uncle Bubba says.

Where is God taking you? What has God told you? What is he speaking to you about the future? What is he asking you to do today? Make that your meditation, your declaration, and your occupation.

Don't forfeit what God gave you because of a feeling. Focus your faith and be strong and courageous.

TWENTY

A GR8FUL HEART IS A STABLE HEART

There's an old Chinese story I really love that is often called the Parable of the Chinese Farmer. It goes something like this.

There was a farmer who lived in a small village in China. One day, his horse ran away. The villagers came by and said, "What bad luck!"

The farmer replied, "Maybe."

A few months later, the farmer's horse returned, and he brought a herd of wild horses with him. The villagers came to congratulate the farmer. "What good luck!"

The farmer answered, "Maybe."

Soon after, the farmer's son was trying to tame one of the wild horses, but he fell off and broke his leg. The villagers came to offer their sympathy. "What terrible luck!"

The farmer replied, "Maybe."

Then a war broke out in the region, and the emperor's soldiers came to the village to recruit young men for the army.

However, the farmer's son was exempt because of his broken leg. The villagers came by again. "What great luck!"

Again, the farmer responded, "Maybe."

That's how the story ends. It could go on forever—and that's the point. You can't really know if something is good or bad, at least not in the moment. All you can really say is, "Maybe."

To me, this story teaches a powerful principle: You can't get your stability from your situation or let your environment frame your emotions. Why? Because you can't see past today. You don't know if the situation will change tomorrow or how circumstances might shift next week. The thing you're griping and groaning about today may be the thing you're grateful for a month from now, a year from now, or ten years from now.

Now, the Chinese farmer could only trust in luck. He could only resign himself to fate. Bad things might turn out to be good things, and good things might turn out to be bad things, and that's the humor in the story. Life has a way of fooling you, of yanking your emotions back and forth, just like those gullible villagers.

Here's the thing, though. You don't trust in luck. You don't rely on the fickleness of fate and fortune. Your faith is in a God who is present in your life and has good plans for your future.

I think that's what Paul had in mind when he wrote, "And we know that in all things God works for the good of those who love him, who have been called according to his purpose" (Romans 8:28). He wasn't saying your life will be free of pain, but rather that it's full of purpose, and even the difficult things will ultimately work together for your good.

That means you don't have to worry and wonder if things are going to work out. You don't have to lose your mind when things go wrong. God's purposes still stand, and sooner or later you're going to see his goodness.

The mindset that "My joy is my job" is based on that truth. It rests on the reality that even when my situation is in flux, my faith is not. It is focused and fixed on a God who knows the future and who will work all things together for good.

Of course, it's one thing to say, "God is working this together for good," but it's another to actually live that way in real time. Your mind can go from peace to panic in a moment. You can go from faith to frustration in two seconds flat. You might be happy and calm one moment, and the next you're saying, "I can't believe they did that again. They are on my last nerve. I can't stand them. Is anybody around here even thinking? Why does this always happen?"

If your sense of well-being depends on something external, it's a setup for instability. There will always be something that comes along and knocks you off-balance because the world itself is not a stable place. You can read twenty-seven headlines and find twenty-seven reasons to believe everything is falling apart and the entire planet is headed to hell. You need a heavenly strategy to keep your emotions in check.

I didn't used to have a process to get my thoughts under control. I tended, for years, to make myself a victim of things

> If your sense of well-being depends on something external, it's a setup for instability. There will always be something that comes along and knocks you off-balance because the world itself is not a stable place.

that were happening on the outside rather than seeing myself as an architect of my surroundings. Instead of understanding what it means to have the mind of Christ, I was stuck in the mind of the flesh: the mental models and thinking patterns of the old me. If something bad happened, or if someone said something unfair or untrue about me, or if I made a mistake, it could derail me for the rest of the day.

I've had to learn that stability happens on the level of your belief system. It comes from the boundaries you place on your inner world. You can't control most of what happens outside your brain, but you can get better at managing what happens inside it: how you interpret events, comments, and situations.

I know we've already talked about this a lot, but trust me, the repetition is necessary. When you're used to thinking about things a certain way, the transformation of your mind requires a consistent training process.

So here's the big question. How do you move from panic back to peace? From frustration back to faith? From instability back to stability?

You and I both know there are many tools and truths that can help: prayer, worship, meditating on the Word, and talking with someone who can help get you out of your funk, to name a few. If you're really brave, you could try an ice bath. Wim Hof says that helps, and in my minor experience with cold plunging, I think he's right.

But for now, I want to focus on the strategy that, for me, seems to make the *most* difference and the *quickest* difference. I'm going to show you a couple of specific ways I apply it too, because I want this to be practical, not theoretical, and because I think it might inspire you to develop your own practice.

The strategy is this: *gratitude.*

I know it's simple, but this is street-fighting stuff, not ivory tower stuff. This is practice, not just theory. It's something you can do when life hits you upside the head and you're saying, "I can't stop the bad thoughts from coming."

A while back, one of my good friends posted something on social media that stuck with me. She was having a horrible day trying to control and corral her small children, and in the video, she appeared to be hiding in a closet. Her video was an SOS. She said something like, "I need help right now! Somebody tell me the best technique you've got to keep from losing your mind when you've been with your kids all day during the summer. Something that won't send me to jail and will work right now. And I don't want to hear, 'The days are long but the years are short.' I need some real-life stuff."

She used a stronger word than "stuff," but you get the point. Sometimes you don't need a slogan or a sophisticated seven-step strategy. Sometimes you need some real-life stuff.

Well, here's the real-life stuff. Here's the best stuff I've got from my secret stash: You can't stop the bad thoughts from coming, so don't try to stop them. Instead, stabilize. And how do you stabilize? Gratitude.

It's the best intervention I've found when I need to bring spiraling thoughts and emotions back under my control. A thankful thought is one of the few things that can match the velocity and force of negative thoughts. It does an end run around the negativity and gets you back to the goodness and grace of God.

This has been life-changing for me. It seems basic, maybe, but it has been so freeing to realize I can decide at any point to vacate a state of anxiety or fear through a practice of gratitude and faith.

I didn't come up with this strategy, of course. You can find gratitude journals on Amazon, gratitude affirmations on Spotify, gratitude teachings on Instagram. But it was in the Bible long before that. For example, Paul wrote, "So then, just as you received Christ Jesus as Lord, continue to live your lives in him, rooted and built up in him, strengthened in the faith as you were taught, and overflowing with thankfulness" (Colossians 2:6–7).

> A thankful thought is one of the few things that can match the velocity and force of negative thoughts. It does an end run around the negativity and gets you back to the goodness and grace of God.

Notice how he says, "rooted," "built up," and "strengthened," which are stability terms, and then he adds, "overflowing with thankfulness." He's saying that stability and gratitude go together. Gratitude isn't the only way to be stable, but it's an important one, it's a reliable one, and often it's the easiest one to grab on to when you need a quick reset.

One exercise I often use is something my daughter, Abbey, and I came up with, actually. It's one of the best things she's ever taught me, right alongside the hidden meanings in Taylor Swift's deep cuts. I've tried gratitude journals with varying degrees of success for years, but sometimes I don't have my notebook. Sometimes I don't want to take notes on my phone because that's where my problem is coming from.

So I'll quickly list, out loud if possible, eight things I'm grateful for right now. Now here's the part Abbey showed me. She taught me to gently trace each of the fingers on my hand with a finger from my other hand as I list them. If you start on the outside of your pinky and go back down on the inside, by the time you get to your thumb, you'll be at eight. It's another layer of tactile symbolism to remind me that every good thing I have comes from God's hand.

Why eight? Because I like wordplay and "eight" is right there in the middle of it. See? GR8FUL.

If that's too goofy for you, I have other reasons. In the Bible, *eight* is the number of new beginnings. *Eight* looks like an infinity loop if you turn it on its side. *Eight* is also the number of legs a spider has, and a spider can spin its own web from the inside. That's the secret of being content, of being strong, of not giving up: being able to find what you need inside of you. You can spin something positive out of nothing. You can spin a better space to live in, regardless of your situation, because what you need is inside you, right where God put it. That's what gratitude does for you.

Pick any eight things, as fast as they come to your mind. Don't analyze your entire past, present, and future and come up with the eight top things. Be more immediate and more granular than that. They can be the simplest things in the world.

The other day I said, "I'm grateful for my wife who wants to go on a date with me tonight." I didn't stop for long, but I thought for a moment about where we might go. That was fun to imagine. It shifted my energy.

"I'm grateful my shoulder didn't hurt this morning like it sometimes does." That mattered to me in the moment. When you get in your forties, stuff starts knocking around. You find yourself thanking God not only for what feels good but also for what doesn't hurt as much as it did yesterday.

"I'm grateful Josh is coming in this afternoon to work on a project with me."

"I'm grateful the sun is out today."

"I'm grateful I get to drive my daughter to school in a few minutes and take her through Chick-fil-A."

"I'm grateful that I'm getting to share this message in a book that will help someone years from now."

"I'm grateful we have a family vacation coming up in a month and everyone seems excited to go."

"I'm grateful for . . ."

It's that easy. It takes three minutes tops. It can be even quicker if you need it to be.

The problem isn't finding eight. The problem is stopping at eight, because once you give your mind something to grab ahold of and gravitate toward, it will keep going in that direction all on its own. It might be a slow start, but notice Paul said, "overflowing with thankfulness." That means once you turn on that faucet, faith keeps coming out. Favor keeps coming out. That's what you want. The goal is to get your mind out of a negative flow and into a positive one.

When you're in an overwhelmed state of mind, don't try to stop the avalanche of anxiety. Meet it with thankfulness. Match it with gratitude. Give your mind something different to grab on to and gravitate toward than the bad things that happened yesterday or might happen today. Your mind can go that direction on its own. Give it an alternate direction. Give it something more constructive to do.

Now, keep in mind that gratitude is not the *only* way to deal with anxiety and other hard feelings, and there might be times you need to do more than a quick gratitude practice. That's up to you because you know yourself the best. I shared earlier that I see a therapist regularly, so I'm a big proponent of taking advantage of whatever strategies and resources work for you, including seeking professional help.

Also, don't use gratitude as a mask to cover up real problems that need to be dealt with. That's a form of spiritual bypassing, which is when you use spiritual language to avoid making practical change. If you need to deal with some stuff, deal with it. If you're called to overcome some problems or face some challenges head-on, don't use gratitude as an excuse to *hakuna matata* your way through life instead of putting in the work.

What I'm saying is that gratitude will help you stop a lot of dark thoughts and feelings before they can spiral into something deeper. That's why I called this street-fighting stuff. It's a strategy you can grab ahold of halfway through a board meeting or while you're standing in line at the DMV, when your mind starts wandering down trails of negativity and you need to find a way back.

I picture my mind as being a little bit like our Boston terrier, Bo. Bo is the dog Holly, Graham, and Abbey begged me to buy for them. It's also the dog that chewed through my favorite Ray-Ban sunglasses just the other day.

What do you do to keep a dog from chewing up your sunglasses? Give him away to somebody else. Just kidding. My kids would kill me.

But seriously, you give him something else to chew on, something that was designed to be chewed on. You distract him by giving him something different to do.

I don't mean to compare your beautiful, capable brain to a Boston terrier, but I think the image fits. At least it does for me. If you don't manage your mind, it will start manufacturing even more negativity, splicing memories together to make painful events even worse and to make you feel more miserable than you already do. It doesn't need any help putting together a H8FUL list of all the things you don't like about your life. Give it a GR8FUL one instead. Get it thinking about the goodness of God, the grace of God, the sovereignty of God who works all things together for your good. Then you can go back to your life, including the things you don't like, and approach them from a higher level.

Use gratitude to engage your faith in God. He is the source of what you have and what you need. You're not just being grateful *for* things: you're being grateful *to* the one who gave them to you. That's something that sometimes gets stripped away when gratitude is taught as a practice. We shouldn't be grateful to the thing; we're grateful to the God who gives the thing. If he takes it away, he can give us another one. There is deep inner stability in that kind of faith.

> You're not just being grateful *for* things: you're being grateful *to* the one who gave them to you.

When should you engage gratitude? Whenever you need it. Actually, even *before* you need it.

I hired a vocal coach to help me manage the wear and tear that years of speaking have inflicted on my voice. One of the first things he did was give me a recording of silly-sounding warmup exercises. These exercises aren't intended for when I feel the pain. If I wait until I feel it, it's harder to deal with. A better plan is to get ready in advance so that when I speak, my voice is strong.

The same goes for my attitude. When should I be grateful? When I need to be, or even before I need to be. Before I snap at someone instead of listening to them, or at least before I snap back for the third time. Before I shut someone's idea down too fast instead of letting it breathe for a bit. Before I feel myself starting to tighten up in my emotions, my mood, or my faith. No matter what situation I am going through or about to face, I can take time to warm up my grateful heart.

You may have been programmed according to a more pessimistic pattern of thinking, always finding what's wrong. You called that being "realistic." But are you being realistic or just reactive? Are you being honest or are you just letting everything around you control you? If you don't overflow with thankfulness, you will probably have a mind that's overrun with anxiety and flooded with fear.

Let me share one more exercise with you. While it's great to thank God for the little things that come to your mind randomly, it can also be helpful to process deeply what you're most grateful for.

Recently, in one of my famous funks, when I couldn't seem to find a single thing that I was doing right in my life, I stumbled upon another gratitude strategy. It started with this question: *If I lost what I love the most, what would I give to have it back?*

The first thing I thought about, and the one I love the most, was God. But I can't lose my relationship with God. So I took it to the human level. If I lost Holly, my wife, whom I love more than any other human being, what would I give to have her back?

The answer came instantly, automatically.

Everything.

I'd give everything to have her back.

Then what do I have right now? Everything. I already have everything. If I would give everything to have her back, and I have her, then I have everything.

Once I started thinking this way, the list kept growing. If I lost my kids, what would I give to have them back? Everything. I would spend every dollar, I would sacrifice every dream, I would go through any inconvenience. I'd give everything to have them back. I do have them, so I have everything. Later that day, when the kids came home from school, I had a less annoyed perspective. Sure, they still fought and bickered and made a mess at the table. But I realized that even in that mess, there was a miracle that too many times I take for granted.

> You have peace with God right now. You have forgiveness of your sin right now. So you have everything.

Now, maybe you *have* lost something you can't get back. I don't mean to bring you pain by including these comments. But even in the greatest loss, I'm sure there's someone or something that comes to your mind that you currently have. What does that relationship or blessing mean to you? And since you have it, how much do you have? How grateful can you be for it?

Beyond human relationships, you have forgiveness of your sin and peace with God. If you lost that, you would give everything to have it back. You have peace with God right now. You have forgiveness of your sin right now. So you have everything.

You have breath in your lungs right now. If you lost your ability to breathe, what would you give to have it back? Everything. So with every breath you take, remind yourself,

"I have everything I need in this moment. I have Jesus. I have the Holy Spirit. My heart is filled with praise."

This doesn't mean that there aren't still unfulfilled desires. It doesn't mean that there aren't painful problems. It's just a perspective to stabilize you when the world seems to be crumbling around you, and it's a strategy to manage your joy.

You choose. Make the shift. The tools are yours to use.

A grateful heart is a stable heart, and a stable heart leads to a stable life. So do it right now. Think of your GR8FUL 8. Say them out loud if you can. Trace your fingers if it helps. Remind yourself of the hand of God on your life.

One . . . two . . . three . . . four . . . five . . . six . . . seven . . . eight.

Go!

TWENTY-ONE

UGLY TRUST

H olly was out of town, and on a whim, I Googled "concerts in Charlotte tonight." I thought I might catch one of my favorite nineties bands on a nostalgia tour, or maybe go see an indie rock show that would make me feel current.

Instead, I ended up at a Mendelssohn cantata.

I was quite proud of myself. I even wore a suit. When Holly called to check in that night, I told her, "You're not going to believe where I went all by myself." She didn't believe it. Not only am I known for being reclusive when given the option, I'm way more comfortable at a rock concert than a symphony.

I had a good time. I was impressed by the musicians. Maybe even a little intimidated by them, too, because they would understand more about music in a coma than I do in my peak state. But beyond all the bassoons and the brass instruments that I probably couldn't correctly identify, there was one thing I couldn't get past: the entire cantata was in German. I didn't know that when I bought the tickets.

Now, I understand that classical music speaks to a lot of people on a subconscious and super-refined level that a punk rock guitarist like me could never fathom, but for me, half of my love of music is locked up in the lyrics. Some people say they don't pay attention to the words, but I'm the exact opposite. Sure, I could follow the emotional thread of the cantata through the music, but without the words, I missed a lot.

Why do I bring this up? Not to brag about how cultured I am—if anything, I think this story is proving the opposite. Rather, it's because I want to highlight a psalm that is very meaningful for me, one I think is very profound in its application for us today, but some of the beauty and message of the psalm are lost in translation.

The psalm is Psalm 34. From a lyrical standpoint, this psalm is a masterpiece. It's an acrostic poem. You can't see this in the English translation, but each verse starts with a different letter of the Hebrew alphabet. When you read it in English, you lose some of that grandeur. You're missing something, just like I did when I sat through Mendelssohn's cantata in German.

At its heart, this psalm is about trusting God *in real life*— not just when you're singing songs in church, not just when things are going well, not just when you feel spiritual and full of faith, but when the world seems to be falling apart around you.

Look at the first four verses. I'm using the King James Version because it sings better.

I will bless the LORD at all times: his praise shall continually be in my mouth. My soul shall make her boast in the LORD: the humble shall hear thereof, and be glad. O magnify the LORD with me, and let

us exalt his name together. I sought the LORD, and
he heard me, and delivered me from all my fears.

There are eighteen more verses that continue in the same
tone. It's inspiring, right? So much faith. So much elegance.
Even without being able to understand Hebrew or admire the
literary craftsmanship, you can see the beauty here.

Why does this matter to us today? Two reasons. First, the
message of this psalm must have been important to David
because he put thought into it. He worked hard on it, and it
shows. It's eloquent, poetic, and expertly crafted. He wants
us to take the message of this psalm very seriously.

Second, it means this was not a spontaneous, real-time
prayer because nobody prays through the alphabet when
they're going through hell. You don't pray artistically orga-
nized prayers when you have a stack of bills in front of you and
you can't pay any of them. You don't pray alphabetic prayers
when your kids are acting like they need three different medi-
cations. You don't craft prayers that are literary masterpieces
when they start firing people who are more qualified than you,
and you're wondering, "Well, if they fired *them*, am I next?"

You cry out. You call out. You say exactly what's in your
heart, and it's not usually pretty.

If you take this psalm at face value, you could almost get
intimidated by how good David is at praise. He seems like
he'd know more about faith and trust in a coma than I would
in my peak state. That's how magnificent and eloquent it is.
But it's a little bit unrealistic if you take it literally.

Who talks like that when they're going through tough
moments? Does anyone bless the Lord at *all* times? Or praise
him *continually*? That's a really high bar. I don't do that. I

listened to Metallica on the way to church the other day. It was early in the morning and I needed something to wake me up, and Mendelssohn just wouldn't cut it. No offense to Felix, but I needed James Hetfield to jumpstart me. I don't think praising God continually means playing only songs from Christian genres.

Not only does David say that he praises God continually, he uses phrases like "I sought the Lord." I don't think I've ever used "sought" in a sentence. I don't ask Holly, "Hast thou seen my running shoes? I sought them diligently, but they are nowhere to be found." When the dumb dog escapes from the house, I don't tell my kids, "Make haste to pursue the brute! Have you sought him at the neighbor's house? Seek him while he may be found."

I don't talk in King James, and I definitely don't pray in King James when I'm going through painful moments. If I bump my toe on the coffee table, I don't say, "Oh, praise the Lord for a coffee table to bump my toe on. Some people in some parts of the world don't have coffee tables or the beans that make the coffee. I bless you at all times, Lord. I bless you for the beans and I bless you for the bumps." In moments like that, the word that comes to mind isn't "sought." It starts with *s* and ends with *t*, but it isn't sought.

Maybe you think trusting God should feel like poetry all the time, but you feel like cussing some of the time, and that doesn't seem spiritual at all. You know you're supposed to be joyful and content, but it's hard to reconcile the bliss you're expecting with the mess you're experiencing.

That's okay. Don't let the devil tell you that your faith is fake just because your feelings are all over the place or you don't see a way forward.

You're putting the wrong kind of pressure on yourself. Because when I say, "My joy is my job," when I talk about how I should be full of God's peace and joy, that doesn't mean my process will always be pretty. Sometimes it's downright ugly.

You've heard of ugly crying? I call this ugly trust. And it's something David was really good at.

Here's the backstory to Psalm 34. David was not yet king. A few years earlier, he had killed Goliath, a giant from the Philistine city of Gath, and he had become a famous

> Don't let the devil tell you that your faith is fake just because your feelings are all over the place or you don't see a way forward.

warrior and a hero of the people. That made Saul, the ego-driven, mostly insane current king, really upset, and he tried to kill David. Understandably, that made David afraid, and he fled for his life.

In desperation, David left Israel, went to Gath, and met with their king, who was called Achish. Now it was the *Philistines'* turn to be afraid, which is also understandable. I'm not sure why David thought it was a good idea for a giant-killer carrying the dead giant's sword to look for help in the giant's hometown. The people of Gath took it as a threat, and rumors and counter-threats started flying.

I think that's interesting. David was running scared, but the enemy was scared of him. Do you know that your enemy recognizes you? Sometimes your enemy knows what you're capable of more than you do. That's not my main point here, but it's something to think about.

David quickly realized his life was in danger. So he did the only thing he could think of doing to prove he wasn't a threat to anyone: he pretended to be insane. He scratched on the doorways and let spit dribble down his beard.

It worked. The king of Gath labeled him a lunatic and let him go.

Put yourself in David's place for a minute. Can you imagine what he felt? He was already under the greatest pressure of his life as he ran from Saul, and then it got even worse when he got to Gath. He was literally about to die. He could see people side-eyeing him and reaching for their swords. It probably wasn't that hard to act crazy because he was at his emotional and mental breaking point already. Then, he had to add humiliation to the desperation. He was mocked, despised, dismissed. He sacrificed his dignity to escape with his life.

And *that's* when David wrote this psalm.

Not while sitting under blue skies and an olive tree while strumming a harp. Not while gazing at sheep grazing by still waters.

He wrote it with spit in his beard and splinters under his fingernails.

So that brings us back to the question: what does it really mean to say, "I sought the Lord"? Because David wasn't praying on his knees in the temple in this story. He wasn't offering sacrifices or burning incense or fulfilling a vow to God. He wasn't reciting alphabetical poems or speaking with King James vocabulary.

He was hiding from Saul. He was humiliating himself before Achish. He was fleeing a madman and feigning madness, all while figuring out his next messy step.

I'm telling you this because sometimes we talk so fancy about faith, but David was scratching gibberish on doorposts

deep in enemy territory when he wrote, "I sought the Lord."
We need to expand our understanding of seeking, trusting,
and believing. These things are messier than we think and
more practical than we may imagine. And we might be better
at them than we give ourselves credit for.

Seeking the Lord doesn't just mean going to church. It
doesn't just mean praying a prayer, singing a song, or reading
a chapter in the Bible. It doesn't just mean you listen to worship music in the kitchen or quote a verse a day to keep the
devil away. I'm not saying you *don't* do those things, but you
can't do those things all the time. Nobody can.

Some days, you're sitting in the doctor's office waiting for
another round of chemo. You're going to couple's therapy and
wondering if your marriage is going to make it. You're trying
to borrow money to keep your business afloat. You can pray
in those moments, but the prayers might not be pretty. That's
okay. That's still faith. That's still trust. It's just ugly trust.

The devil might try to tell you that your faith isn't real
because you're at your breaking point. I would argue that it's
the most real it's ever been. You're in that space between calling out to God and seeing his answer.

That's a hard place to be. Remember, though, that one of
the most beautiful psalms in the Bible came from one of the
ugliest situations. David sought the Lord with spit in his
beard. Some of the most beautiful testimonies in your life
will start with ugliness. Ugly emotions. Ugly options. Ugly
steps.

Ugly *trust*.

You might be wondering why I'm talking about trust in a
section that's about joy. Here's why. "Owning your emotions" doesn't mean just thinking happy thoughts all the

time. You're not Peter Pan trying to fly. Owning your emotions means you give yourself space to feel all the emotions, but you don't let them define you. You admit them but you don't submit to them. You feel *and* you trust. You fear *and* you believe.

David knew this. He said God delivered him from all his fears. Wait a minute, David. Fears? I thought you had faith. Which is it? Were you blessing God or stressing out? Were you writing songs or wondering if you were getting out of this alive? Was that praise in your mouth or drool on your beard?

Yes and yes.

It was both.

It was all of it.

Trusting in God doesn't mean you will never have fearful thoughts. Seeking God does not mean you will never feel like you're going crazy. The truth is nobody knows what you are really going through. Nobody knows what you have to push through. Nobody knows how close you came to quitting, how much you struggle with feeling like you're enough, how hard it has been for you to fight for these fourteen months of sobriety, how much grit it takes to keep showing up at your job, how tense and difficult the situation has been in your home.

Nobody else knows, but God has heard you. When you cried, he heard. When you prayed, he heard. He heard, and he is going to answer. He is going to deliver you. You will see his faithfulness. You don't know how or when, and you don't know what steps you'll go through to get there, but God does.

So don't feel guilty about feeling scared while you're following God. Don't look at your fear and criticize your faith.

Don't think that just because you're desperate you're letting God down. That's not hypocrisy; it's humanity. It's ugly trust.

Remember, David wasn't talking so poetically and peacefully while he was going through all that stuff. He was mumbling like a madman. He was acting crazy, and he probably wondered if he was going crazy—and he called that whole crazy process "seeking God."

So don't wait for pretty. Pretty is acrostic poems and King James prayers. Pretty is symphonies and orchestras. Pretty is when you see the answer and rejoice in the deliverance. The time will come for pretty, and it will be beautiful.

Right now you need practical. Practical is doing the *next best thing* because you can't do what you really want to do. The Bible says that later, David was still fleeing Saul, and he thought to himself, "One of these days I will be destroyed by the hand of Saul. The best thing I can do is to escape to the land of the Philistines. Then Saul will give up searching for me anywhere in Israel, and I will slip out of his hand" (1 Samuel 27:1).

So David went to Gath for the *second* time. Remember, the first time, he was seen as a threat because of his giant-killing fame and his close connection to Saul. Now, though, things had changed. He had been a known outlaw on the run from Saul for a long time, so he wasn't a threat. If anything, he would have been seen as an ally because the Philistines didn't like Saul either.

I can only imagine the emotions he must have felt as he walked through the city gates again, though. This wasn't where he wished he could be. It wasn't where he wanted to build a house and raise his kids. That's why he called this step, "the best thing I can do." It wasn't really the best thing, because the best thing would have been to return to his home in safety. But it was the best thing he could do *considering the circumstances*. When he said the best thing, he really meant the second-best thing, or the next-best thing.

That's how David sought the Lord. By doing the next best thing. "Next best" means two things at the same time. It means David did the second-best thing, because the best thing wasn't an option. And he did the next thing, he took the next step, because he couldn't just give up.

He sought the Lord *by* taking steps. His actions were the proof of his faith. They were his unspoken prayer.

> It's road-weary, battle-scarred, tearstained, drool-in-your-beard trust, but it's still trust. It's still faith. It's still hope. It's still praise.

That's how you seek the Lord too. That's how you trust him. Sometimes that's all you can do. You do the next best thing you can do, even when you wish you could do something better, even when you can't see the end of it, trusting that God will guide you as you go.

It's ugly trust.

You're stressed, but you're still seeking. You're tired, but you're still trusting. You're worried, but you're still pushing forward, looking forward, taking steps of faith as best as you know how. It's road-weary, battle-scarred, tearstained, drool-in-your-beard trust, but it's still trust. It's still faith. It's still hope. It's still praise.

And someday, like David, you're going to say, "I sought him when I couldn't see him. I was groping around in the dark, feeling my way forward in faith, but I couldn't feel him. I sought him, and there was a space, and for a while I wondered if I would make it, but he heard me, and he delivered me."

For David, there was a seven-year space. Not seven days. Not seven months. Seven *years* that Saul chased him. Seven years that he made his home in caves. Seven years that he dealt with fear and depression. This story in Gath was one incident of many. He didn't just seek the Lord one time. He had a lifestyle of turning to God, leaning on God, following God. He did a lot of next best things in that time. He lived in over a dozen places during the years he outran Saul. He was often just one step ahead, and it was exhausting. There were times he thought he was going to die. But he didn't quit. He trusted.

Have you been there? Are you there right now in some area of your life? Maybe you're awaiting a legal verdict. Maybe you're trying to find a place to live. Maybe you're working through a relational conflict. You can't see the solution and you wonder if God knows or cares.

That's when trust comes in. That's when your faith rises above the level of your emotions. It's when you commit your way to the Lord. It's when you plan your steps but let the Lord direct your paths. It's when you do the next best thing.

Three months from now, you might be writing acrostic poetry about all that God has done. You might be telling someone your testimony with tears of joy in your eyes. But right now, it's ugly. Right now, you can't see the end, so you just need to do the next best thing.

"I would love to be taking my kids to school every day, but I only get to see them every other weekend. So, when I get them, I'm going to make it count, because that's the next best thing."

"I would love to have somebody to take long walks on the beach with, but I don't have somebody, and I don't have a beach, so I'm going to get on this treadmill and get a podcast and take myself on a walk, because that's the next best thing."

"I would love to be further along in my finances by now, but I didn't do it all right, and some things blindsided me along the way, so I'm going to do the next best thing, and I'm going to start managing my money now."

What's the next best thing you can do? That's all you have to do. You don't have to figure out the next fifty things. That's God's job.

> Humility is not demanding to be in control and in the know all the time, but rather taking the next step in obedience to God, trusting him to lift you up at the right time, in "due time."

It's going to be ugly sometimes. But do you know what "ugly" stands for to me? *Until God Lifts You.* U.G.L.Y. I even have a verse for that. "Humble yourselves, therefore, under God's mighty hand, that he may lift you up in due time. Cast all your anxiety on him because he cares for you" (1 Peter 5:6–7).

Humility is relying on God to do what only he can do, and it's doing what he says you can do. Humility is not demanding to be in control and in the know all the time, but rather taking the next step in obedience to God, trusting him to lift you up at the right time, in "due time."

God will lift you up in *due* time. So what will you *do* in the meantime?

This might not be a season of pretty, but it can still be a season of praise. It can still be a season of prayer. It can still be a season of trust. It might be ugly praise and ugly prayer, but that's okay. It might be spitty-beard, crust-in-your-eyes, tears-on-your-pillow, sleepless nights trust, but that's alright. You know that when you seek him, he hears you. When you cry out, he is listening.

So you can say, "I will bless the Lord at all times. I trust you, God. I trust you with my future. I trust you with my family. I trust you with my children. I trust you with this decision. I trust you with this economy. I trust you with this move. I trust you with this transition."

Whether you're spitting and scratching, or whether you're composing lyrics of praise, it's still trust. It's still prayer. It's still seeking.

And soon, in due time, in God's time, you'll be able to sing with David, "I sought the Lord, and he heard me, and delivered me."

He will lift you up in due time. What will you do in the meantime?

Sometimes we overlook the fact that God didn't just create emotions—he *has* emotions. He is emotional, and we were made in his image. It's no wonder emotions play such a big role in our lives. God isn't bothered by your emotions, or confused by them, or frustrated with them, like I often am when they show up in my teenage kids. Instead, God is the perfect father who wants to help you get the most out of your emotions. That's the heart behind the mindset "My joy is my job." You can find stability and peace in God, and you don't need to deny your desires and feelings in the process. Your joy is your job, but your God is your source.

In light of this knowledge, what's the next best thing you can do *right now*? As we move into the sixth and final mindset, we're going to look at ways to "embrace your now." How do you take the next best step? How do you do the thing that you would do? This last mindset is one that will set you up for success in whatever season or situation you find yourself: *God has given me everything I need for the season I'm in.*

GOD HAS GIVEN ME EVERYTHING I NEED FOR THE SEASON I'M IN.

ACTION STEP:
EMBRACE YOUR NOW.

TWENTY-TWO

LOOK TO THE LEFT

Recently I received a note from a young man in my church named Trenton. Trenton is twenty-three years old, and he has cerebral palsy. He serves on the greeter team at our Lake Norman campus every other Sunday. Everyone who knows him says that his energy is infectious.

He wrote to let me know how much a recent sermon of mine and a song that we had written had encouraged him. The song was called "More Than Able," and in the sermon, I preached what I shared earlier about God commanding Gideon to "go in the strength you have."

Trenton told me that the sermon was deeply meaningful to him. He said, "I have a disability. That's how people define me. But when you preached about Gideon and you said, 'go in the strength you have,' I realized something. If you take the word *disable* and put *go* in front of it, it spells 'God is able.' Even though I may be limited from a human perspective, God is able to do great things through my life."

That is such a beautiful truth, and it spoke to me when I read the note. Trenton may have a physical limitation, but he has developed incredible spiritual strength. Where others see a disability, he sees God's ability, and that's what matters most. Trenton sees the fullest, most accurate perspective of himself.

Do you have that perspective? Can you see that version of you? Do you see the ability of your God or the disability of your debt? Of your illness? Of your failure? Of your lack? We all have limitations that we think could keep us from seeing God do great things in our lives. Instead of letting them stop us, we need to let his "go" turn whatever is disabled into "God is able."

This willingness to trust God's grace in every situation lies at the heart of the mindset "God has given me everything I need for the season I'm in." Gideon experienced that grace, as we saw in previous chapters, and many other heroes in the Bible did too. When they stepped out in faith, they saw God's perfectly timed provision for every circumstance.

I want us to look at another hero in Judges who was uniquely prepared for his role. His name was Ehud. Ehud's story is not usually taught in Sunday School, and there's a reason for that. It's really gruesome. It's not something you want to read while eating.

At the time Ehud came on the scene, Israel had been under the power of Moab for eighteen years. They had to pay an annual tribute, and Ehud was in charge of carrying this tribute to the Moabite king, named Eglon.

The first thing the Bible tells us is that Ehud was a left-handed man. That's an important detail. In that culture, left-handed people were often considered less-than-ideal soldiers.

Ironically, Ehud was from the tribe of Benjamin, which literally means "son of my right hand." So in a sense, Ehud didn't fit into his own tribe, and he didn't fit the mold of a warrior.

Ehud must have been fed up with Moab's dominion, so he decided to take matters into his own hands. Into his *left* hand, to be precise. When it came time to take the tribute to Eglon, he crafted a homemade eighteen-inch dagger and hid it under his cloak, against his right thigh. Then he went to meet with King Eglon, who, the Bible specifically mentions, was a very fat man. Imagine Luke Skywalker confronting Jabba the Hutt.

After Ehud turned over the payment, he told the king he had a secret message for him. So Eglon ordered everyone out. As Ehud came close to the king, he reached across his body with his left hand, pulled out the dagger, and buried it deep in Eglon's stomach. The king didn't see it coming because it came from the left.

This is where it gets really gory. The Bible says that the fat of Eglon's belly closed over the dagger, swallowing it entirely, and his bowels discharged. Ehud locked the door, left the body where it fell, and sneaked out of an upper room. How? Apparently by crawling down the king's private toilet, which probably would have emptied into a chamber pot below. Then he escaped unseen. They might have smelled him, but they didn't see him. He went out and raised up an army, led a revolt, and freed the land from Moab's power.

Why am I telling you all this? Not to ruin your appetite but to illustrate a point: *God often does things in an unlikely way.*

In a secret way.

In a way nobody saw coming.

In a moment no one expected it to happen.

Using somebody no one thought could do it.

I want you to ask yourself: *What is the secret weapon God has put in my left hand? What is the secret weapon God is turning me into?*

In other words, what is the unexpected thing God wants to do through you? What is the unexpected way he wants to meet your needs? What is the unexpected skill he's given you? What is the unexpected situation you are going to be the solution for?

Maybe you're going through some challenges and you have a certain expectation of how things need to resolve. Maybe you've even been praying very specifically, telling God exactly how he could fix this or solve that. But what if you're looking at this the wrong way? What if you're looking at the wrong things to help you? You're waiting for right-handed strategies and God made you left-handed. Maybe you already have what you need, but you've just been looking at the wrong hand.

I'm sure Israel was looking for a flamboyant leader with a foolproof battle strategy and a fancy army. Instead, they got a left-handed loner with a DIY dagger and an escape plan borrowed from the Teenage Mutant Ninja Turtles. Nobody saw that coming.

And that's why it worked.

Only Ehud could have pulled that off. And only you can pull off what God is calling you to do.

That's why you can't compare yourself to anyone else. You can't write yourself off by saying, "Oh, *they're* the right person. They do it the right way. Look how smart they are. Look how charismatic they are. Look what their parents taught them. Look what they inherited. They're the obvious choice."

You don't know what God wants to do with you. They've got all this stuff in their right hand that you don't have, but God has put something in your left hand, and nobody will see it coming. The enemy won't know what hit him. Stop talking about what you don't have in your right hand and start looking to the left. They might be "right" according to what is expected and normal and obvious, but if God is looking left, their right is wrong.

You have to believe that God is looking at *you*. He has prepared *you*. He is calling *you*. The misfit. The left-handed person from a right-handed tribe. He's looking at what he put in you, at what he gave you, at what he is asking you to use now.

That's what the mindset "God has given me everything I need for the season I'm in" is all about. It's not about just barely making it to the end of the month. It's not about kicking back and expecting God to do all the work. It's about stepping into what this season demands of you by leaning into *who God made you to be*. That's what the new you would do.

Say it out loud, if you can: "God has given me everything I need for the season I'm in." Emphasize "everything" and "season" when you say it because those are the keys to this mindset. You don't have everything you'll need for every season, but you have what you need for this season, so embrace your now. Instead of getting paralyzed by the future and by what you don't have and can't do, get energized by your now as you focus on what you *do* have and *can* do.

Ehud must have gotten energized at some point. He started looking around his house trying to figure out what he could turn into a weapon, and he came up with an eighteen-inch blade. He realized the left-handedness that people always laughed at was his secret strength. He drew up a plan worthy of a *Mission Impossible* storyline, plotting his escape through a toilet because nobody would ever think to stand guard over a chamber pot.

It was genius. Gross and graphic and gory, but genius.

I wonder, what genius is within you? What could you come up with if you looked around at what you have? If you redefined your quirks as qualities? If you took on a new energy and applied Holy Spirit creativity to whatever you're facing?

Midian ruled for eighteen years until Ehud got fed up. Do you need to get fed up with something? Maybe you *could* figure out a strategy to get out of debt. You *could* reconcile with your mother. You *could* solve the morale problem with your employees. You *could* connect with your junior high son who suddenly seems distant.

> God has given *you* what you need for *this* season. It's in you because he put it there, but you have to see it.

You might not do it the way everyone else does, and that's your genius. That's why you can pull this off. God has given *you* what you need for *this* season. It's in you because he put it there, but you have to see it. You have to value it. And then you have to use it.

I'm not saying it's easy. I'm just saying you have a unique perspective. You have your own creativity. You have specific skills and experience and knowledge, and God gave those to you on purpose. He wanted you to have them. He knew the seasons you'd go through, and he knew what you needed for each one.

It's interesting to me that the Bible doesn't say God anointed Ehud with the Spirit of the Lord. It doesn't even say God told him to do what he did. It just says he did it. I'm not saying he acted foolishly or that what he did was wrong. I'm just saying that God doesn't always announce what he's doing when he's doing it. Sometimes you won't even know he's doing anything at all. Sometimes you're just doing your best, doing the next best thing, and God shows you a path nobody else could have seen. Then one thing leads to another until you see an unlikely victory in an unexpected way.

So don't be so quick to write yourself off just because you aren't like everybody else. Don't diminish what makes you different. Destiny is often hidden in your difference.

Often when we're going through something difficult, we want God to do something dramatic. But what if he's already given you what you need, you just haven't seen it yet? What if you're scanning the horizon, waiting for a right-handed rescuer, but God already gave you a left-handed anointing?

> **Destiny is often hidden in your difference.**

Now, when I talk about your left hand, I'm not just referring to your obvious strengths. That's part of it, but what I really mean is that God uses a wide variety of unexpected, unlikely, unforeseen things to bring about deliverance. Sometimes those are your unique skills—but other times, they are your unique *weaknesses*. Or at least what you perceive to be weaknesses.

I'm not a boxer, but I took one lesson, one time, and one thing stuck with me. The instructor showed me that because I'm right-handed, I should lead with my left foot. That seemed counterintuitive. My left side is my weak side, so my left foot is weaker, right? It's less coordinated. It's less balanced. But he explained that you pivot off your weak leg so you can punch with your strong hand. The power comes from the back. It comes from an unseen place, a place that doesn't seem strong on its own—but the power is in the pivot.

The metaphor I see is that often God will lead with something that looks like weakness because your power is found in his pivot. He has us take steps forward, even in our weakness, then his right hand does the work. I love what God told Paul when he was frustrated with his weakness: "My grace is sufficient for you, for my power is made perfect in weakness" (2 Corinthians 12:9).

> God often does things that are hidden from view. They are unexpected and unseen, but that doesn't make them unimportant.

Where are you stepping out and it feels like weakness? Where is God asking you to lead with the left? Maybe you're in a role at work you don't feel prepared for. Or you just had a baby and you know you aren't the parent you wish you could be, at least not yet. God's right arm will do the work. Just lead with the left. Lead with what you have. "Whatever your hand finds to do," the Bible says, "do it with all your might" (Ecclesiastes 9:10). It might not feel like strength, but God's power is backing you up.

Sometimes God does something unexpected through us or for us, and we think we just got lucky. "Wow, I'm glad that worked out! That was a close call. What a coincidence!"

But God's sovereignty has been there all along. Coincidence is his pseudonym. It's a name he goes by when he doesn't want you to know it's him yet. Coincidence is just God in a costume. So when God starts answering your prayer, get used to being surprised. Not just by what he does, but by what *you* do.

Notice that everything in this story is built around the idea of secret. Being left-handed was a secret strength. The dagger was a secret weapon. Ehud claimed he had a secret message. He killed Eglon secretly, he locked the door to keep the assassination a secret, and he escaped through a secret exit.

God often does things that are hidden from view. They are unexpected and unseen, but that doesn't make them unimportant. It doesn't make them insignificant.

Isaiah, one of Israel's greatest prophets, had a season where he felt hidden. Listen to how he described it.

> Listen to me, you islands;
> hear this, you distant nations:
> Before I was born the LORD called me;
> from my mother's womb he has spoken my name.
> He made my mouth like a sharpened sword,
> in the shadow of his hand he hid me;
> he made me into a polished arrow
> and concealed me in his quiver.
> He said to me, "You are my servant,
> Israel, in whom I will display my splendor."
> But I said, "I have labored in vain;
> I have spent my strength for nothing at all.

> Yet what is due me is in the LORD's hand,
> and my reward is with my God."
>
> (Isaiah 49:1–4)

Isaiah said, "He hid me; he made me into a polished arrow and concealed me in his quiver." He was hidden because he was significant. It was a sign of careful preparation for an intended purpose.

Sometimes we think that being hidden is a sign of insignificance. If people aren't celebrating us or people aren't recognizing us, we don't feel validated. "Nobody knows me. Nobody sees what I can do. I only have three hundred followers on Instagram." Gideon only had three hundred followers and he took out the entire Midianite army. Followers don't make you valuable. Being celebrated doesn't make you significant.

You're not insignificant. You're *hidden*. There's a big difference. God is doing something subtle in you. He's sharpening and polishing you. You're hidden in this season, but your purpose will be made plain in due time. God is getting you ready so that in that season, you'll have what you need. Just as you hide valuables in your home so thieves can't steal them, God has things locked inside of you because they are valuable. It's your treasure, the resource of your contribution, your spiritual gift, your acts of service. When the time is right, he is going to bring you forth.

It's interesting that Isaiah saw himself as a weapon for God's use. It was the same with Ehud. Ehud didn't just *have* a concealed weapon; he *was* the concealed weapon.

And so are you.

The things God has put in you and the grace he has placed on you are not random. They are not minor things. They are there for a purpose, and you are here for a purpose. He made you left-handed because he wants to do a left-handed miracle.

You are the weapon.

You are the secret thing God is doing.

You need to see yourself that way.

If that's a surprise to you, it just proves how sneaky God is. He's been working on you in secret so he can do something powerful in public when the time is right.

The issue of timing is crucial, though. Isaiah knew he was a weapon, but he also felt frustrated when he didn't see results. That's why he said, "I have labored in vain; I have spent my strength for nothing at all." I'm sure Ehud felt the same way every year, every time he trudged to the enemy's palace to hand over Israel's hard-earned tribute. He had to wait for the right time, for God's time, which wasn't necessarily the expected time.

> The things God has put in you and the grace he has placed on you are not random. They are not minor things. They are there for a purpose, and you are here for a purpose.

Do you feel that way? Maybe it feels like you've invested your labor, but it's been in vain. You made yourself vulnerable trying to create relationships, but it backfired. You tried so hard to get over that health challenge, but nothing has improved. You tried to break out of that toxic pattern, but you keep going back to it. Your sacrifice feels like it was made in vain because nothing changes, nobody sees you, nobody thanks you, nobody promotes you.

But keep reading. Isaiah isn't done yet. "Yet what is due me is in the Lord's hand, and my reward is with my God."

What hand? Sometimes it's the left one. Sometimes it's the unexpected hand of the Lord. The miracle you didn't see coming. The gift you didn't know he put in you. The door you almost didn't knock on, but you did, and it changed everything.

What is due you is in the Lord's hand because *you* are in the Lord's hand. He is polishing you and hiding you for his purpose. Other people might have written you off. You might have written yourself off. But you're not forgotten. You're just hidden.

Don't let lack of progress turn into self-pity. Self-pity feels good for a minute, but it distracts you and discourages you. It steals your confidence and kills your creativity. It turns you into a victim when God is calling you into battle. It sabotages the strategic side of your mind, the problem-solving part that sees potential in hidden daggers and unguarded toilets.

You might be hidden, but things are still happening. Secret doesn't mean static or stale or stagnant. Maybe you're a stay-at-home parent and you feel forgotten, but you're putting values in your kids, and they're going to be strong, healthy people because of your investment. Maybe in some area of life God is using you in an imperceptible way to shift something. You don't see it yet, but he does, and your faithfulness is having an effect. Maybe you're doing things that seem so natural to you that you barely notice them or brush them off as insignificant, but your contributions will bear fruit for years to come.

Only you could do what you're doing, and you need to know that. Don't despise the left-handed skills. The left-handed strategies. The left-handed risks. The left-handed plans. The left-handed miracles. Don't assume the "right" way is the right way. It might be right to you but wrong to God.

He's doing something unexpected, something the enemy didn't see coming and won't be able to stop. It might not have happened yet, but it will. You'll see it, and you'll be part of it, if you learn to look to the left.

TWENTY-THREE

HELP ME FAIL

One time a bodybuilder came over to my house, and he was working out with my boys and me in the Pound. The guy was in his early twenties, and he was in the best shape of anyone I have ever met in my life. He brought his girlfriend along, who was also a bodybuilder. I figured I'd take the opportunity to ask him for some hacks so I could look like him—preferably ones that didn't involve human growth hormone.

He said something that left a lasting impact on me. It was a phrase he repeated throughout his workout, and it stood out to me more than any tip he could have given me. When he was getting ready to approach his last few reps on every set, he would say to his girlfriend, who was spotting him, "Help me fail."

I thought it was interesting that he said it that way. He didn't say, "Help me get one more rep." He didn't say, "Help me finish the set" or "Help me set a new PR." He might have meant all those things too, but what he said was, "Help me *fail*."

When you think of things you want people to help you do in life, that's not on the top of the list, is it? You don't call up your accountant and say, "Hey, help me fail to submit my taxes this year." You don't hire a coach to help you with your golf swing and tell him, "Help me add a few points to my game." You don't hire somebody to tutor you in school and say, "Help me go from a C to an F."

That obviously wasn't the kind of failure this bodybuilder wanted. He wanted the kind of failure that would make him stronger on the other side.

I'm not a weight-lifting expert, but I've been lifting long enough to know that resistance training works by tearing down the muscle fibers and stimulating muscle growth and nerve connections. "Help me fail," in this guy's weight routine, meant "Help me get to the end of what I can do right now because that's where growth and change are going to happen."

Now here's my question. When you're facing pressures or problems that feel like a crushing, heavy weight, do you have faith that God could help you fail? Do you have faith that he is giving you what you need for this season, even when it feels like you're strained to the breaking point?

To be honest, I don't ever pray to fail. I say, "God, help me succeed. Help me win. Help me accomplish more." It's okay to want to win. The Bible says that God leads us in triumph, that we are more than conquerors, and that we should run in such a way as to win the prize.

But winning doesn't always mean what we think it does. For God, character growth is a win. Perseverance is a win. Getting rid of old ways of thinking and acting is a win.

And sometimes to win, you have to fail.

You have to go through things that break you down in order for God to build you up.

What does this have to do with the mindset "God has given me everything I need for the season I'm in"? Doesn't having everything you need mean you should never fail?

> You have to go through things that break you down in order for God to build you up.

Yes and no.

On one hand, it means that God is faithful to be with you, to strengthen you, to lead you, to deliver you. So no, you don't need to fear failure in the sense of utter destruction. Proverbs says, "For though the righteous fall seven times, they rise again, but the wicked stumble when calamity strikes" (24:16).

But on the other hand, God will often take you to the end of yourself because that's where your strength starts to grow. The fact that he is with you and that he provides for you, though, gives you *a safe place to fail.*

That's an amazing gift. But you have to look at it that way or you'll never take advantage of it.

Often, we are too scared of failure. We think that getting to the end of ourselves is a terrible place to be because it's so uncomfortable. But for God, that's where growth begins.

You don't need to literally pray, "God, help me fail!" but you do need to know that you *will* fail—but even in failure, God is giving you all you need for the season you're in. As a matter of fact, he might be giving you what you need *through* your failure.

I hate that! I'm not going to lie and say I love to learn from my mistakes. As I said earlier, I'm a perfectionist at heart. I don't like failure. I wish I could get every decision exactly right on the first try. I wish I would never have to apologize for goofing up again.

It's not going to happen, though.

So I'm learning to give myself space to grow in the safety of God's grace. I'm learning to recognize that even when I fail, God is enough, and I am enough, because he's keeping me safe and helping me improve.

The Bible says, "We also glory in our sufferings, because we know that suffering produces perseverance; perseverance, character; and character, hope" (Romans 5:3–4). You don't feel strong when you fail, but when you fail, he makes you stronger. That's grace.

Now, I'm not talking about going shopping for suffering. Suffering doesn't make you spiritual and martyrdom doesn't make you mature. Sometimes we try to make our life harder, even subconsciously. We shop for suffering, then we tell ourselves stories about the situation we're stuck in and make our suffering even worse.

Don't do that. That's not helpful. There's enough pain built into the normal patterns of life. You don't have to go looking for it.

What I'm saying is that when pain and difficulty come your way, give yourself room to learn through trial and error. Allow yourself space and grace to fail, but do so in a way that brings you out stronger on the other side. Fail forward into your future.

When those heavy situations that feel like they're too much come your way, you can say, "God, help me fail, because I'm not getting it right in every area of my life. I'm not getting it right in the way I'm parenting. I'm not getting it right in the way I'm running this business. I made this decision, and it felt good at the time, but now it completely backfired. God, help me fail. Move me forward."

If you're heading into a situation this week where you feel like you're not enough, don't let fear of failure paralyze you. Maybe it's a person who you know is not going to accept you. Or a discipline you can't stick to yet like you want to. Or a project at work you've never done before. Or a schedule that is so full you know you're going to let somebody down.

Whatever it is, *be more committed to progress than perfection.* Remember that you are being built up through the very things that feel like they're tearing you down.

If you're going to succeed, you have to risk temporary failure. Yes, it feels horrible in the moment, but it's working in your favor. It's a failure that carries you forward.

Jesus called himself the Good Shepherd, but you could call him the Good Spotter too, because he helps you fail. There is safety in his presence. He won't let you drop this weight. He's going to keep you safe and make you strong.

He's not going to carry it for you either, because you are enough for this. You have what you need for whatever you're facing. He's not only standing behind you, he's living inside you, and he's saying, "You've got this. I'm with you. This is making you stronger. It's building you back bigger. I'm giving you what you need for the season you're in, but you have to step into it. You have to accept the challenge. You have to push yourself to the limit, and if you fail it's okay because I'm here to help you."

Remember Peter walking on water? That wasn't exactly a resounding success. Peter said, "Jesus, if you tell me to come, I'll come." Jesus told him to come, and Peter probably wished he would have kept his mouth shut. But to his credit, he gave it his best shot, and he did pretty well for his first attempt. And when his faith faltered, Jesus was right there.

Peter gets a lot of flak for that, but he *walked on water* while the other guys stayed in the boat. Regardless of whether it was his impulsiveness or his faith that motivated the action, he learned a firsthand lesson that the other disciples could only observe from a distance.

Notice something, though. Jesus taught him about faith *after* he attempted to walk on water. He had to get wetter before he got wiser. There are some lessons that can only be learned the hard way. Through mistakes. Through trial and error. That's not a bad thing, though. Peter failed, but he learned, so he didn't actually fail. The sinking was temporary but the growth was permanent.

I think many of the greatest steps we take look a lot like Peter walking on water. We step out, we falter, we call out, we learn a little, we try again. Meanwhile, other people sit in the boat and critique our technique. They are dry but dormant. They are safe but stagnant. Wouldn't you rather sink a little today so you can grow a lot tomorrow?

> Let God help you fail as you grow, and help you grow as you fail.

Put yourself in a place where failure isn't just an option: it's a normal part of the process. Let God help you fail as you grow, and help you grow as you fail. That means getting out of your comfort zone. It means doing things that feel difficult or unnatural. "I asked for forgiveness, but I did it imperfectly. God, help me fail. I tried to be present at dinner, but I checked my phone three times. God, help me fail. I tried to stay calm in that situation, but I still got a little stressed out. Help me learn from my mistakes. Help me fail."

Don't fear your mistakes, your weaknesses, your limitations. If you let God be strong through them, you'll grow because of them. Failure done right is not failure at all. It's just another step forward as you do the new you.

TWENTY-FOUR

FOUND FISHING

I listen to a lot of motivational speakers, fitness gurus, and the like while I'm driving or working out, and one thing they often talk about is how the right morning ritual can set you up for success. One morning, not too long ago, I was feeling a little unsettled, a little anxious. So I started going through a list of all the morning routines and rituals I had heard about that are supposed to get you back on track for the day. I wrote them down, just for fun, and by the time I finished the list, I had to laugh at myself. I thought, *Steven, you need to stop watching YouTube videos and listening to audiobooks about morning routines. This is out of control.*

If I did all those things—the breathing, the biblical meditation, the cold and hot showers, the prayer lists, the acts of generosity, the exercise, the silence, the balanced breakfast, the vitamin supplements, the to-do list, the gratitude journal—I wouldn't finish my morning routine until three in the afternoon.

I felt God speak to me, though. "Steven, you have an abundance of things that you know to do to get to a better place. Pick one. Do one."

Pick one, do one.

It's a simple thought. But it's a powerful one. "I have an abundance of things I could do. I will do one right now."

It comes back to the idea "do the thing that you would do." What is "the thing" for you in your current circumstances? If you're feeling stuck, or moody, or worried, or confused, or ashamed—what is something that could get you back on track?

You can't do everything, but you can pick something and do it. That is how you embrace your now: by accepting where you are and doing what you can with what you have. Maybe it's just a quick attitude adjustment before you head off to work. Maybe it's reaching out to set up an appointment with someone you know will give you good advice. Pick one, do one.

> Faith isn't knowing the whole journey ahead or being certain about what you're supposed to do next.

In a sense, those choices *are* faith.

Faith isn't knowing the whole journey ahead or being certain about what you're supposed to do next, but rather it is being faithful with what you have at hand and putting yourself in a place where God can find you, encourage you, use you. I wouldn't call it meeting him halfway—it's more like meeting him about five percent of the way in. But that five percent matters. That's your position and posture of faith. It is evidence that you believe God is with you and that he has given you what you need in this season.

When I don't know what to do in a particular situation, I try to remind myself that when I make a move, God makes it clear. I'd prefer it the other way around—I want God to make it clear, and then I'll make a move. But it often doesn't work that way.

Are you in that place right now? Maybe you're saying, "What can I do? What should I do? I don't know. I just don't know." I've been there. We all have, many times. Sometimes all it takes is a bad mood, a bad decision, or some bad news to leave you feeling overwhelmed and hopeless. You lost your job at the worst possible time. You didn't get into the degree program you were planning on. You had unexpected medical bills for the third month in a row and now you're in a financial hole.

How do you respond when you don't see a path forward? How does the *new you* respond? Because that's the version of you that you want to carry forward.

The old you might have frozen up. It might have demanded an explanation and a road map. It might have fallen into self-doubt or self-pity. The new you, though, embraces your now, knowing that God has given you everything you need for the season you're in. The new you asks, "What can I do right now? What do I know to do? What has God shown me? I'm going to pick one thing and do it."

You have to be willing to do what you can to keep moving, even if the destination is a little uncertain and the road to get there seems shrouded in fog. God probably hasn't given you a detailed ten-year plan in every sphere of your life. Instead, he's asking you to be willing to take the next faith step forward, and then the next one, and then the next.

Maybe you've read the story in John 21 about how Peter went fishing after Jesus' death and resurrection. He invited some of the other disciples along, and they fished all night. Early in the morning, Jesus found them fishing, revealed himself to them, and cooked them breakfast. Then he started talking to Peter. Remember, after Jesus was arrested, Peter had denied three times that he even knew him. Now, as they stood next to the fire, Jesus asked Peter three times if he truly loved him, and he told him three times to feed his sheep. It was a dramatic, emotional scene.

Peter gets a lot of criticism for going fishing because that was his occupation before Jesus called him. I've heard preachers say that he gave up and went back to his old way of life and he dragged other people with him. I don't think that's true, though.

I don't think he went fishing out of fear. I think he was fishing in faith. He wasn't giving up. He was reaching out.

Think about it. I'm sure he was emotionally raw. After all, he had denied Jesus publicly and then fled in fear when Jesus and the disciples needed him most. He failed utterly at his leadership role. But he wasn't the kind of guy to hide or mope, so when he didn't know what else to do, he did what he was doing when Jesus first called him to be his disciple. He did what he knew how to do, and he trusted Jesus to find him there.

Remember, Peter had a history of seeing miracles come from this lake. It's where he cast his net on the other side of the boat and caught so many fish that his nets began to break. It's where Jesus came to his disciples walking on the water, and Peter took a couple of steps on the water himself. It's where Jesus told Peter, when he was worried about paying taxes, to go catch a fish, and that fish came out of the water with money in its mouth.

So when Peter went back to his boat after Jesus' death and resurrection, I think he was fishing in faith. He was fishing *for* faith. When he was caught in a place between failure and calling, between fear and his future, between who he used to be and who he knew he was meant to be—he went fishing.

That was exactly where he needed to be. Jesus found him fishing.

Can you relate? Maybe you've found yourself saying, "I don't know what to do. I don't know if God can still use me. I don't know if I've ruined my reputation. I don't know if everything I've done was for nothing. I don't know if God really forgives me. I don't know if I can go forward now that I've seen I'm not as strong as I thought I was. What do I do?"

What if you said, "I want to be found fishing"? What if you said, "I don't know what to do, but I'm going to do the thing that puts me closest to where I've met God before"?

That's what Peter did. His attitude was, "I'm far from who I need to be. I don't have any idea where I'm going next. But I'm going back to the boat because I remember when Jesus called me. I'm going back to the thing that I know how to do, and I'm going to trust God to show up. I'm going to do what I know while I wait for him to show me what I don't know."

> What if you said, "I don't know what to do, but I'm going to do the thing that puts me closest to where I've met God before"?

When Peter did what he knew, Jesus did something new. Not only did he restore Peter, gently and firmly, but he expanded his calling. "Feed my sheep," he said. The encounter with Jesus happened not in spite of the fact that Peter went fishing, but *because* he went fishing. Jesus showed him the next steps after Peter took the first step.

Here's the point. When you feel confused or overwhelmed by something you're facing, don't freeze up. Don't get analysis paralysis. You don't have to understand every detail or see every step ahead.

Instead, go fishing.

What does that mean? It means doing what you know you should do, even when—*especially* when—you don't have control over everything else in your life. What things do you already know how to do? What things do you have at hand? What do you know God wants you to do now?

Pick one. Do one.

That's fishing. That's faith. That's a posture of curiosity, of exploration, of openness. That's where God will find you, and it's where you'll find what you need to keep moving.

Sometimes this means taking a big step forward, but often it's just an attitude change. That's why I mentioned morning routines that get your mind and emotions in the right place. I'm not saying you must have a specific routine— I'm just saying that even when you're overwhelmed, you have options. You don't always get to choose how your day flows, but there are ways to start off on the right foot. And, if things go sideways, there are ways to stop and catch your breath. There are ways to recapture momentum.

For Peter, that was fishing. For me, it's often practicing gratitude, such as the Gr8ful 8 exercise I mentioned earlier. "I'm grateful for the time I had with Elijah lifting weights today. I'm grateful Graham and I got to watch wrestling this weekend. I'm grateful Abbey gave me a hug and told me she loved me last night. I'm grateful Holly and I are going on a walk today, and for once it's not twenty-two degrees out."

When I do that, suddenly the day has a different feeling. All because I went fishing for gratitude. I went fishing for faith. I went fishing for a perspective shift. I found *them* fishing, and Jesus found *me* fishing.

Here's another "fishing" strategy I use. This is something I do when I feel blocked because it opens me up to possibilities and breaks me out of my inertia. I call it "wills, cans, and mights."

First, I quickly list all the *wills* that come to mind, which are things that people would do for me if I asked them to. "Holly will go on a walk with me and give me feedback on this idea. Chuck will oversee that project. Robert will give me a tennis lesson."

Then I list the *cans*, which are the things that I could do if I wanted to. These are within my own power. "I can make a list of possible topics to preach about next week. I can text that person and set up a meeting."

Finally, I list the *mights*, which are tentative things that I may or may not want to follow up on. "I might go to that concert. Eric might have lunch with me this week."

That's it. It takes maybe five minutes. The goal isn't to solve problems, but rather to embrace my now and to open myself up to possibilities. By the time I'm done, I've identified some things I *don't* need to be worried and distracted about, and I've identified a few others that I could tackle next. It's a simple strategy to get past mental and emotional blocks and figure out what is actionable right now.

How about you? How do you get unblocked? How do you move from pessimism to possibility? From resenting your now to embracing it? Where do you meet with God? Where do you hear him best? What is one thing you could do *right now* to get closer to him and closer to the new you that God is guiding you into?

In other words, how could you go fishing?

If you don't go fishing for the right things on purpose, you'll likely end up fishing for the wrong ones by default. If you fish for reasons to give up or reasons to be discouraged, you'll catch them. If you fish for offense, you'll find it. If you fish for excuses, they'll bite quickly.

But on the other hand, if you fish for kindness, you'll find that too. If you fish for reasons to believe, or if you fish for the best in people, or if you fish for the next thing that God is giving you to do, you'll get it. You get what you fish for, not what you wish for.

So go fishing and see what you catch. See what God does. See what he shows you.

> Are you spending more time telling God how big your mountain is than telling your mountain how big your God is?

That means taking time to seek God about what to do next, no matter how small it might seem. Some of us spend more time looking for something to watch on Netflix than we do searching the Spirit of God to see what his will is for today. When was the last time you got alone with God and asked him for a strategy to get you moving again? When was the last time you asked somebody in your life for help, or have you allowed pride to keep you paralyzed? Are you spending more time telling God how big your mountain is than telling your mountain how big your God is? Instead of sitting around feeling bad about your failures or worrying about what's coming next, get up and go fishing.

Jesus will find you there. He is reminding you, "I'm glad you're going to be out on that boat because that's where I'm going to be this morning. I'm going to be on the lake looking for somebody who's doing what they know to do so I can show them who they really are."

God has given you everything you need for the season you're in. Don't stress or obsess over every possible permutation of your future. Work on today. Get in your boat today. Look for Jesus on the waters of faith today. Make the most of what he has given you. Embrace your now and be found fishing.

TWENTY-FIVE

GOD CHOSE YOU ... WILL YOU?

Side by side in my refrigerator, I have bottles of water and bottles of Diet Coke. Every day, I get to choose which one to put into my body. Usually I go for Diet Coke, if we're being honest. Don't judge me.

Side by side on my phone, I have my Bible app and my YouTube app. I get to decide where to put my focus and time. It's my choice.

Side by side in my mind, I have thoughts that encourage me and thoughts that paralyze me. There's a voice that says, "You have something to say. You can help people. You can encourage people." And there's another voice right next to it that says, "You don't have everything all figured out. Who are you to tell people how to live?" I choose which voice to listen to. It's up to me.

And side by side, there is my old self and my new self. The old me and the new me. The me I've always known, and the me God knew since the foundation of the world.

Which will I choose today?

Which will *you* choose today?

I don't think you have a clue how much choosing you actually do in a given day. I know I don't. But I'm beginning to learn the extent to which my life is built around decisions. Earlier I quoted Psalm 118:24. "This is the day the LORD has made. We will rejoice and be glad in it" (NKJV). God made it, but I decide what to make of it. That's a choice.

The power of choice is the heart behind all six of the mindsets we've been exploring together. It's the heart behind this book. It's the heart behind the action step "embrace your now." You can't control most things, but you can control the most important things: your mind, your emotions, your words, your reactions, your decisions, your internal dialogue.

Most of the choices we make are small and almost instantaneous. When I see my daughter in the morning, I choose whether to greet her enthusiastically—"Hey, Lucius!" (that's her nickname)—or whether to be distracted or grumpy. To be honest, I have a very mixed batting average when it comes to the tone of my voice.

When I initiate a work-related conversation, I choose whether I begin with, "Hey, I'm excited about . . ." or whether I skip right to the thing I'm frustrated about. I decide if I'm going to approach tasks from negativity or from possibility.

The other day I had a conference call about a project we were working on. Thirty seconds before I got on the phone, I asked myself, *How do I want to show up on this call? At what level do I want people to engage?* I decided I wanted to go into the call with positive energy. That's not my default, in case you haven't figured that out yet. My default is to present problems and then try to solve them before I will allow myself to feel hopeful and happy. But I defied my default, and it felt good. It felt right.

I started out with, "Hey, everybody, I have good news and better news, but I have to give you the good news first, because the better news won't make sense without the good news." It changed the tone of the entire conversation. The positivity didn't make the call less effective than it would have been if I showed up saying, "Well, I have bad news and worse news." It made the call *more* effective. It brought a creative force into the conversation that moved things forward.

Every morning, I have to decide which version of me I'm going to send into the world. Will it be the me who wants to be happy right now at all costs, or the me who will thank me in ten years for making the right decisions today? Will it be the me who makes me cringe when I see it reproduced in my kids, or the me they can be proud of, feel safe around, and come to for advice when life gets crazy?

Pre-coffee me is not the me I want the world to see. When I first wake up, my breath isn't the only thing that's bad. My attitude is bad. So are some of my emotions and thoughts. I have to get my head in the right place or I'll have a meltdown by ten o'clock. As I said earlier, I have to take a few moments to reflect on what I have or I'll obsess all day over what I don't have. If I don't adjust my mindset in the morning and believe that "God has given me everything I need for the season I'm in," I'll start the day in a deficit. I'll run around feeling like I don't have enough strength, I don't have enough energy, I don't have enough resources.

Which version of you are you sending into the world every day? Is it the one that will get you where you want to go in your career, your family life, your health, and your walk with God? Is it the one that comes from abundance? Is it the one that believes in a God who does more than you could ask or think? Are you choosing to be who God says you are and do what God says you can do? Or are there scenarios where you are settling for immaturity in the name of authenticity, where you're stuck in the old self when God is calling you to put on a new self? Are you consistently choosing the new you?

Now, it would be really easy to follow this train of thought down a rabbit hole of shame and self-doubt. You make thousands of decisions a day, and you're not going to get them all right. I'm not telling you to obsess over every choice you make, every word you say, every emotion you feel. I'm just saying that the launchpad for *doing* the new you is *choosing* the new you. It's accepting who God made you and then making the daily—sometimes hourly—decision to walk in the fullest version of that. We've spent this entire book exploring how to do that on a practical level. Each mindset is a tool, a strategy, so you can decide to do the next best thing even when life is confusing or overwhelming.

It's easy to believe in yourself when you're on a winning streak, but how do you choose the new you even when you don't feel like you can? When you're more aware of your weakness than your potential? When you're more conscious of your mistakes than your gifts?

Choosing yourself must start and end with the fact that *you are chosen by God in Christ*. Ephesians 1:4 says, "For he chose us in him [Christ] before the creation of the world to be holy and blameless in his sight."

God didn't just know you before he created you. He *chose* you before he created you.

Peter was chosen by Jesus, even though he would go on to curse and deny that he knew Christ. In the same way, *you* were chosen even though *you* cuss and do some other bad stuff. That doesn't give you permission to continue with bad habits, but it gives you power to overcome them by knowing that God knew all about them, and he chose you anyway.

Get this deep down: God chose you.

God has options. God can call anybody he wants. God can use anybody he wants. He could have gotten any vessel he wanted, but he picked you. The Bible calls us "chosen vessels." That means you are a

> Choosing yourself must start and end with the fact that *you are chosen by God in Christ.*

handpicked vessel of God even if you feel stubby or misshapen or too tall or too funny-looking. You're a chosen vessel even if you have a broken handle. You're a chosen vessel even if you have a few cracks.

The poet and singer Leonard Cohen said there's a crack in everything; "that's how the light gets in."* Our weaknesses and our cracks are where God's grace and glory shine through. That's where God does his best work. Sometimes we get obsessed with the container—with our bodies, our skills, our titles, our fame—but God sees right through those things. They aren't deal-breakers at all. They are part of our beauty.

Now, I'm all for taking care of your physical appearance. I'm all for improving your financial health. I'm all for growing your skill set. But to make those changes in a healthy, balanced way, you have to know deep down that God chose you.

---

* Leonard Cohen, "Anthem," *The Future* (music album). Songwriters: Leonard Cohen; Anthem lyrics © Stranger Music Inc. (1992).

"Yeah, but I'm not . . ." You're *chosen*.

"But I did that . . ." You're *chosen*.

"It's just that they . . ." You're *chosen*.

You have been selected and accepted by a God whose sovereignty supersedes every situation and every human limitation. Your unique atomic construction was the handiwork of the author of time and space and galaxies. The God who architected the caterpillar to become a butterfly has created you for good works. He has called you for a special purpose. He has predestined you by his love. He has adopted you as a son or a daughter. He has brought you into his family.

> You have been selected and accepted by a God whose sovereignty supersedes every situation and every human limitation.

That's good news, isn't it? It means 5'6" was supposed to be 5'6". It means that beneath whatever you don't like about yourself radiates a spirit that is uncontaminated by comparison to others.

"I wish I had been born in the 1800s. That would have been cool." You weren't, and you weren't supposed to be. It's not as romantic as it sounds. They didn't even have toilet paper back then. You were supposed to be born now.

"I wish I could have lived in a simpler time. I wish I could have walked the earth with Jesus." You can't. You're walking now. The Bible says God appointed the times and places where people should live. He called you to this time, he called you to your family, he called you to your disposition, he called you to make the most of your personality. That's all part of his purpose.

Remember, God chose you before the creation of the world, and that means he chose you before life got messed up or you got messed up. He chose you before you got a divorce. He chose you before you had those sexual relationships. He chose you before you got trapped by that addiction. He chose you before you made that mistake. He chose you before you were abused by that person. He chose you before you blew that opportunity.

God chose you—but you have to choose yourself.

Stop rejecting who you are or who you are not. Stop comparing yourself to people you don't even know. Believe what God says about you. Decide to act like the person he says you were created to be and step into the calling he created for you.

We already saw that you were "created to be like God in true righteousness and holiness," as Ephesians says, but you have to reach for it, moment by moment, in every situation. I don't mean that you have to strive for it or earn it; I mean you reach for it like you're receiving a gift from God, or like you're getting a Diet Coke out of the fridge. Or a bottle of water, if you're in a healthy mood.

What do you need to reach for and receive? And in order to do that, what do you need to release and leave behind?

God chose you, so you have to let go of all of the reasons why he shouldn't have. You have to stop reciting all of the excuses you make for why he can't use you. Remember how God told Moses to deliver his people from Egypt, but Moses said he couldn't speak well enough? Or how God told Gideon he would save his people, but Gideon said he was the weakest warrior in all of Israel? Or when God said Sarah would have a child, but she laughed out loud in unbelief? They were holding so tightly to their excuses that they struggled to receive God's empowerment.

You and I do that sometimes. "I don't have the time. I don't have the money. I don't have the skills. I don't have the intelligence. I don't have the background."

Release that and reach for what God has given you. Choose to believe who God says you are. "I choose to believe that Jesus Christ has made me righteous. I choose to believe that the Holy Spirit lives within me. I choose to walk in it. I choose to flow in it. I choose to turn the other cheek in this situation. I choose to walk past that offense. I choose to forgive. I choose to speak life. I choose to go forward."

God chose you. Now, will you choose you? Will you embrace the true you?

This isn't always easy. It's definitely not instantaneous. I struggle with this, and I'm sure you do too. I choose the horrible attitude sometimes. I choose the gossip, which feels good going down but then burns in the pit of my stomach because I can't look people in the eye if I've been talking badly about them behind their backs. But I recognize that's not the me I want to be at all. I don't want to be the bad-attitude me, the backbiting me, the petty me.

I want to be a bigger me. I want to be big enough to look at somebody and see that they have pain, they have feelings, they have reasons, they have dreams, they have goals. I want to see people as people, not as problems to solve or tools to use. I want to see the gifts in my kids rather than getting side-tracked by the little things that trip me up in their everyday behavior. I want to see their intention. I want to see the seeds of what God has put in them. I want to see them as God sees them, and I want to see me as God sees me.

That's who I want to be, but I have to choose to be it. I have to choose me.

And you have to choose you. You have to settle deep in your soul that God saved you, God loves you, God is for you, God is with you, God has called you, God is guiding you, God is changing you.

Will you choose yourself?

Will you choose not to abandon yourself to the addiction? Will you choose to reach out to somebody you love today rather than isolating yourself and staying in your head? Will you choose to move forward on that big dream you have, even if it's just a tiny step in the right direction? Will you choose the future instead of the past? Will you choose to be present instead of being distracted? Will you choose growth even when it's hard work?

I'll say it again. God chose you. *Will you?*

Maybe you're in a place where you want to quit on yourself right now. Maybe you want to give up on ever being free. Maybe you want to give up on maturity. Maybe you want to give up on discipline. Maybe you want to give up on becoming more balanced. Maybe you want to give up on receiving healing.

But if God won't give up on you, you don't get to either.

If Jesus went all the way to the cross for you and endured the cross, despising its shame, and sat down at the right hand of God, you can endure as well.

It may take a little longer than you hoped. It may hurt a little more than you expected. But the God who chooses you is asking *you* to choose you today.

He knows what you're going through—but he also knows what you're capable of. Do you? He knows what you're missing—but he also knows he has given you what you need for the season you're in. Can you see it?

What I love about the mindset "God has given me everything I need for the season I'm in" is that it doesn't just point to today. It points toward the future. You have enough for this season, *and* you'll have enough for tomorrow's season.

Jesus said, "Therefore do not worry about tomorrow, for tomorrow will worry about itself. Each day has enough trouble of its own" (Matthew 6:34). That was a dark but humorous way of saying God knows what you need and when you need it, and he'll make sure you have it.

Regardless of what is around the next bend in the road, you can rest in the knowledge that you'll have enough, and you'll be enough. God already knows the season you'll step into tomorrow, the challenges you'll face a year from now, the doors he's going to open in ten years. You might not, but he does, and his provision will be there when you get there.

STEP BY STEP, DAY BY DAY

I was talking with a friend of mine recently, and he said, "Man, isn't it supposed to get easier at this point in our life? Is it still going to be this much of a battle every day?"

I knew what he meant. When I was in my twenties, I assumed that by the time I hit my forties I would have things all figured out. My biggest battles would be behind me, and the future would be easier. The right thing attitude would be more automatic. The right thing to do would be apparent.

Turns out I was wrong.

Turns out there are always some unexpected, overwhelming challenges around the next bend. Turns out there's a difference between struggling with something and surrendering to it. Turns out there are still things about myself that can and should change. There are mistakes I need to make, skills I need to learn, "demons" I need to deal with, and doors I need to walk through with courage and tenacity.

Turns out God isn't done with me yet.

And he's not done with you either.

That's an awesome thought. It means you aren't locked into your present. It means your best days are not behind you. There are still mountains to climb and battles to win and dreams to fulfill.

Psalms says that God's thoughts toward you outnumber the grains of sand and that your days are recorded in his scroll. That means he has a bigger vision for you than you do. He trusts you more than you do. He believes in you more than you do. And he won't give up on you like you sometimes do.

Remember, though, as you walk forward into the new you, there is a lot riding on who you let into your head. Your stability and your inner peace depend on whether you tune in to God's voice above all the noise, or whether every rumor, threat, and vain imagination has access to your ear.

The old you would have been swayed by those negative voices, but I believe the new you is learning to focus on the voice of God. You are learning to listen to the one who knows you best and sees you as you were created to be.

I'm not saying you should refuse to listen to other opinions or to ask for advice. I'm just saying that if you want to do the new you, you can't listen to every opinion or criticism you come across. The wrong voices are the ones that don't know the new you but still think they can tell you who you are and how much you're worth. They are the voices that point out your problems and magnify your mistakes, not to help you grow, but to hold you back. To lock you into the version of you they have always known, instead of encouraging you to grow into who God made you.

Sometimes those voices are real people. But more often than not, they are internal voices. They are memories. They are imaginations. They are insecurities. They are mental models you've adopted and adapted and accepted over time. They are tricks for kids, lying lizards, dead weasels.

The six mindsets that we've explored in this book are meant to replace those voices. Instead of listening to the things that hold you back, you have the power and the potential to change your inner dialogue and to adopt a God-focused mindset. No matter what challenge or battle or opportunity you face, you can do the thing that the new you would do, because that is the real you.

Let's look at the six mindsets one more time. If you can, say these six mindsets out loud to yourself, one at a time, with all the conviction and faith you have. This is the voice of the new you. This is the way the new you thinks, talks, and responds.

1. *I'm not stuck unless I stop.*
   Action Step: Commit to progress.

2. *Christ is in me. I am enough.*
   Action Step: Accept your Self.

3. *With God there is always a way, and by faith I will find it.*
   Action Step: Focus on possibility.

4. *God is not against me, but he's in it with me, working through me, fighting for me.*
   Action Step: Walk in confidence.

5. *My joy is my job.*
   Action Step: Own your emotions.

6. *God has given me everything I need for the season I'm in.*
   Action Step: Embrace your now.

I hope you'll even put these six mindsets on sticky notes and post them somewhere you will see them in the moments you need them most. Sometimes they won't feel true. Sometimes they'll seem like wishful thinking. But these are the words God has spoken over your life. They are as true in the valley as they are on the mountaintop. They are as true when you're doubting as they are when you feel certain.

Hear the Holy Spirit whispering them into your heart right now.

God is with you.

God is for you.

God chose you.

Will you?

ACKNOWLEDGMENTS

Justin Jaquith, you were the ideal creative collaborator to bring this book to life with me. You possess a rare combination of big picture consciousness and relentless meticulousness. You dove to the bottom of the Basin. And you did it the right way, which wasn't the easy way, until we discovered and captured the energy and essence of this message. Thank you for being tenacious and patient, flowing with a preacher, and staying all in, to the end.

Shannon Marven, you expanded my concept of what an agent can be. You brought a level of support and nurture that comes only from someone who cares deeply. Thank you for really believing in me and helping me get through precious and break through to personal.

Jan Miller, thank you for your vision and commitment to my next step.

Daisy Hutton, Beth Adams, Patsy Jones, and the team at FaithWords, I am excited to be publishing with you. You are excellent partners.

Lindsey Newton, you are an anointed archivist. Thank you for stewarding the recording and distribution of my sermons faithfully for so many years.

Lindsey Pruitt, Chad Zollo, Cherish Rush, and Christy Collins, I wish every pastor could have a team like you. Thank you.

Chunks Corbett, I know you probably won't read this whole book, but hopefully you get this far, because if not for you, it wouldn't exist. Thank you for never letting me forget this is part of my calling too. Thank you for every time you've blocked for me so that something creative could be born.

Holly Anna, you insisted there were more books in me, and you did more than say that. You made sure I found my next one and made sure it didn't stay inside. That's what you always do. Thank you. You are the greatest gift God ever gave me.

ABOUT THE AUTHOR

STEVEN FURTICK is a pastor, *New York Times* best-selling author, and Grammy® Award–winning songwriter and producer. As founder and senior pastor, he has helped grow the multi-site Elevation Church into a global ministry through online streaming, television, and the music of Elevation Worship. He holds a master of divinity degree from Southern Theological Seminary and is the author of *Crash the Chatterbox*, *Greater*, *Sun Stand Still*, *(Un) Qualified*, and *Seven-Mile Miracle*. Steven and Holly live in Charlotte, NC, with their two sons, Elijah and Graham, and daughter, Abbey.